DATE			

CHAUCER AND THE
CANTERBURY TALES

CHAUCER AND THE CANTERBURY TALES

By

WILLIAM WITHERLE LAWRENCE, 1876—

BIBLO and TANNEN
NEW YORK
1 9 6 9

Copyright 1950 Columbia University Press

Reprinted 1969 by arrangement with Columbia University Press

by

Biblo and Tannen Publishers, Inc.
63 Fourth Avenue   New York, N.Y. 10003

Library of Congress Catalog Card No. 72-79514

Printed in U.S.A. by
NOBLE OFFSET PRINTERS, INC.
NEW YORK 3, N. Y.

TO THE COLUMBIA STUDENTS OF
FORMER YEARS WHO HAVE EXPLORED
THE MIDDLE AGES WITH ME

❧ PREFACE

THIS BOOK, the plan of which is set forth in detail in the introductory chapter, has been written for those who are interested in the *Canterbury Tales* as literature, but have no leisure to struggle with a mass of technical criticisms in order to gain a firm foundation for appreciating its artistry. Thoughtful readers will, I think, like to know something of the way in which such a foundation must be constructed, and of the difficulties to be surmounted in the process. In deciding disputed questions, I have occasionally been obliged to differ from distinguished authorities, but I console myself with the reflection that those authorities are themselves often in lively disagreement. Less attention has here been given to the individual tales than to the structure and design of the whole, and less to contemporary pilgrimages, which have already been carefully studied, than to the artistic use which Chaucer made of them. A constant effort has been made, for the benefit of those who do not know the Middle Ages well, to emphasize the differences between the habits of thought of the fourteenth century and of our own day.

The following pages will, I hope, also be of some interest to the specialist. They embody a good deal of first-hand research, most of which has not appeared in print. In general, I have tried to be conservative. When I have advanced new ideas, I have tried to make it clear that they are my own. Some matters have been emphasized which will seem to the expert trite and obvious. My experience as a teacher has been that for a wider audience such matters cannot be neglected.

Since the main emphasis here is upon literary art, the apparatus of scholarship has been subordinated. Full and detailed references, as in a technical monograph, would not only clog the main discussion, but increase greatly the size of the volume in a day when typesetting and paper should not be wasted. Excellent bibliographical assistance, carefully classified, lies ready to hand elsewhere. That a book or article has not been mentioned in the text, notes or bibliography does not mean that it is not important, or has been overlooked. This bibliography makes, of course, no claim to completeness; it is intended only to provide suggestions for reading and consultation in connection with the matters here discussed. The following abbreviations have been used in the notes in referring to periodicals, the year of publication being added for ready reference: PMLA, *Publications of the Modern Language Association of America;* MLN, *Modern Language Notes;* JEGP, *Journal of English and Germanic Philology;* MP, *Modern Philology.*

I am especially indebted to Messrs. Houghton, Mifflin and Co. for permission to use in citations the text of F. N. Robinson in the "Cambridge Poets" series, and to reprint some editorial comments; and also to quote from R. K. Root's *Poetry of Chaucer.* Acknowledgments are also due the following publishers, details being given on the appropriate pages: to Messrs. Little,

Brown and Co. for a quotation from J. P. Marquand's *H. M. Pulham, Esq.;* to Messrs. Henry Holt and Co. for extracts from J. M. Manly's edition of the *Canterbury Tales* (1928) and his *Some New Light on Chaucer;* to Rinehart and Co., for quoting from G. K. Chesterton's *Chaucer* (Farrar and Rinehart, 1932); and to the University of Chicago Press for quoting from the Manly and Rickert *Text of the Canterbury Tales.*

My colleague Professor William T. Brewster very kindly read this book in unrevised form in manuscript. Wise counsel has been given by old friends who are no longer living, Professors Carleton Brown, Jefferson B. Fletcher, and especially John S. P. Tatlock. These critics must not, of course, be held responsible in in any way for my conclusions. The librarians of Harvard University and Dartmouth College have kindly loaned books. Professor Charles H. Livingston, of Bowdoin College, has verified references to Old French texts.

For some thirty years I read the *Canterbury Tales* annually with a graduate class in Columbia University. Their comments have often proved of great value in writing about Chaucer, and their enthusiasm was a constant stimulus.

W. W. L.

Portland, Maine
February, 1949

↤§ CONTENTS

CHAUCER AND THE
CANTERBURY TALES

Go, litel book! God sende thee good passage!
Chese wel thy wey; be simple of manere;
Loke thy clothing be lyke thy pilgrimage,
And specially, let this be thy prayere
Un-to hem al that thee wil rede or here,
Wher thou art wrong, after their help to cal
Thee to correcte in any part or al.

Sir Richard Ros, *La Belle Dame sans Mercy*

ᘺI. INTRODUCTION

I N A COLLECTION OF VERSE published in the year before
his death, nearly a hundred years ago, Walter Savage
Landor suggested in an interesting way the qualities
for which Chaucer is read in modern times by an ever-
increasing number of admirers. A fastidious classical
scholar, Landor emphasized the "fun" of traveling with
the master to Canterbury, the "merriment" of the *Tales,*
the lovability of the poet's personality, and the feeling
that he seems alive despite the passing of the centuries.
Unlike many medieval writers, Chaucer is the most com-
panionable of men, the right kind to enjoy in hours of
relaxation, for the "fun"—and much else—that is in him.
Such is the ideal way to read the *Tales,* the way Chaucer
must have intended they should be read, the way we
ought to read them today.[1]

The handicaps to such enjoyment are all too familiar.
More than five centuries separate us from the days of
Richard the Second. Everything has changed—social and
political organization, religious beliefs and observances,
manners, customs, and conventions. The language requires interpretation, and the delicate music of Chaucer's
verse escapes us unless we learn to read it aright. Quite
as great have been the changes in the art of poetry, in the
relation of poet and audience, and in the effects produced

---

[1] Walter Savage Landor, *Heroic Idylls, with Additional Poems*
(1863). For quotations see Caroline F. E. Spurgeon's excellent *Five
Hundred Years of Chaucer Criticism and Allusion, 1357–1900,* II
(Part 3), 68. References to other evidences of Landor's interest in
Chaucer will be found in her index.

by different types of literature—matters which must have special attention in the pages that follow. Allusions familiar to a man of the fourteenth century have in many cases no meaning for us without special study. Moreover, various technical problems are still far from a definite solution. We cannot even be sure of the sequence in which Chaucer meant the tales to be read.

There is no lack of guidance. The research of the last half century has been truly extraordinary, and it has been carried out with the most minute attention to detail. Hardly any aspect of the life and letters of the fourteenth century has remained untouched, and Chaucer's career and the significance of his earlier work for the *Canterbury Tales* have received the most careful attention. But the layman may well be appalled by the very richness of the evidence and the multiplicity of eager interpreters. Thus H. D. Sedgwick, in a volume intended for the general reader, and pleasant for its enthusiasm, compared Chaucer specialists to the members of an exclusive club—"when they come to publish their dissertations, comments, criticisms, and suggestions, they often fail to remember that persons outside this club do not understand what they are talking about." [2] Professional scholars have frankly recognized this. H. S. Bennett, of Emmanuel College, Cambridge, observes in the *Oxford History of English Literature* that "it is particularly ironic that this most humane of English poets should be in peril of being buried under a mass of erudi-

[2] Henry Dwight Sedgwick, *Dan Chaucer*, New York, 1934, p. 20.

tion." [3] And J. L. Lowes, a man who united in a remarkable degree exact scholarship and keen literary appreciation, "suspected" that "it is . . . the awe-inspiring *che-
vaux de frise* of technical Chaucerian scholarship which
has often scared the laymen for whom Chaucer wrote
from entrance upon their rights." [4]

At the same time it is clear that subjective and impressionistic criticism has sometimes erred in ignoring the
results of research which often seems "dry" and technical. It is easy to fall into that error. Chaucer astonishes us
again and again by his modernity. His humor, one is
tempted to say, is like nothing else in the Middle Ages,
and a sense of humor is a wonderful solvent of the barriers imposed by time. He is so great a poet, his human
sympathy is so pervasive, his knowledge of mankind so
profound, his personal attitude toward the reader so
intimate, that one easily gets to feel that the secrets of his
art may best be understood by entering into close com-
munion with him and throwing distracting commentaries aside. Two of the brightest and best of our creative
literary artists may serve as illustrations. G. K. Chesterton, in a substantial book, asserted, with disarming frankness, that he was writing for those knowing even less
about Chaucer than himself and that "it is possible to
know him without knowing anything about him."
There is the doctrine, in good round terms. Chesterton's

[3] H. S. Bennett, *Chaucer and the Fifteenth Century*, Oxford, 1947,
p. v.

[4] John Livingston Lowes, *Geoffrey Chaucer and the Development
of His Genius*, Boston and New York, 1934, p. 6.

book is delightful, like everything he wrote, but it is rather a pleasant excursion for the initiated than a safe guide for the uninformed. What he tells us "about" Chaucer—and there is a good deal of this—is not always right, and sometimes has a very real effect upon literary appreciation. His picture, with its pleasant whimsicality and love of paradox, is occasionally out of focus, like the Prioress's little dogs, fed on the daintiest food, which are in his pages miraculously transformed into greyhounds.[5] Some of the finest verse of the present Poet Laureate of England has been written under the influence of the *Canterbury Tales,* and Masefield's admiration for the poet is obviously deep and sincere. He is less

[5] G. K. Chesterton, *Chaucer,* New York, 1932, *passim;* see pp. vii, 205. The reader is told that Chaucer began the *Canterbury Tales* "in his comparatively crippled and limited old age . . . something like a shabby old pensioner," sitting at his window and looking out at the Abbey, where his tomb was to be (p. 154). This contradicts our best knowledge. It is commonly held that the poet "began" the *Tales* about 1387, when he was between forty and fifty years old. He was very far from senile retirement. He had recently been made Justice of the Peace for Kent, and Knight of the Shire. In 1389 he was appointed to "the important and responsible office" (Robinson) of Clerk of the King's Works, and later to that of Deputy Forester of the royal forest of North Petherton (renewed as late as 1398), which was certainly no sinecure. Chesterton thought that he probably regarded the Canterbury collection as a kind of postscript to the *Troilus* (p. 161). Rather a long postscript—a project for some hundred and twenty tales, not including the prologue and the narrative of the pilgrimage! He did not take a lease on a house in the precincts of the Abbey until the year before his death, some twelve years after he seems to have begun work on the *Tales* as a collection. (Quotations by permission of Rinehart and Co.)

happy in criticism; his little book on Chaucer [6] shows the danger of treating a medieval poet according to modern standards. In it we are given several imaginative reasons why Chaucer chose to write the *Tales* in verse rather than in prose (excepting, of course, the *Melibeus,* the *Parson's Tale* and the *Retraction*). No doubt a poet can best divine what goes on in the mind of another poet, but here the simple and obvious reason is that in the fourteenth century verse was the commonest medium of story-writing in England and that Chaucer had always employed it for that purpose. Homiletic, didactic, and informational writing, on the other hand, was likely to run into prose, as the portions of the *Tales* just mentioned, the *Boethius* and the *Astrolabe* illustrate. Again, we are told that Chaucer's "merry and bawdy" tales were written in verse because the language and rhythms of prose were inadequate for his purpose. But we are not told the important fact that the narrative type from which these tales were imitated, the fabliau, was in verse. And we should always remember, as J. W. Mackail has reminded us, that "such prose as had been created for Italy by Boccaccio, supple, succinct, lucid, was not yet available in English."

Discussion of the relative importance of appreciative and historical criticism, of the subjective and the objective approach—which indeed cannot be kept wholly separate—has been going on for a long time, and will no doubt continue long after the daisies are growing over

[6] John Masefield, *Chaucer,* New York, 1931.

our heads. It would be useless to linger over the question here. But upon one point there can be, I think, little difference of opinion: that the further we recede from our own times, the less can impressionistic analysis stand by itself, no matter how penetrating the imagination behind it. We cannot make allowances for the archaisms in Chaucer's language and verse and then treat him as if he had been a contemporary of Tennyson. Much more is needed. The odd conviction that ignorance of the results of technical study of the Middle Ages is no bar to understanding the essentials in a poem of the fourteenth century must pass, I believe, into the limbo of critical curiosities.

The proper realization of what research can teach us is, of course, no easy task. A vast deal of chaff must be threshed from the wheat before the wheat can nourish us. Just here, however, is where scholarship can perform a very real service, and—to change the figure— take a wider view, and place the best results of its own labors in the proper perspective to aid us in entering into the magic world of Chaucer's imagination.[7] It is sometimes impossible to effect a compromise between conflicting points of view; the writer must decide according to his own best judgment, and trust that he may enjoy the reader's confidence. William James once wrote that "the

[7] This has already been done, for various aspects of his art, by Kittredge, Root, Lowes, Robinson, Legouis, French, and others, but much remains to be accomplished. I have attempted to sum up the best results of technical study for the literary appreciation of *Beowulf* in *Beowulf and Epic Tradition,* Cambridge, Mass., 1928, 1930. The general method there employed is followed in the present volume.

wisest of critics is an altering being, subject to the better insight of the morrow, and right at any moment, only 'up to date' and 'on the whole.' " [8]

Interdependence between appreciation and research is particularly necessary with Chaucer's maturest poetry. Comprehension of his earlier pieces does indeed require exact knowledge of conditions and traditions now forgotten by all save the scholar, but the problems in these pieces are seldom of great complexity. The case is very different with the *Troilus* and the *Canterbury Tales*. Into these the poet poured the richest treasures of his life and art—into the former with greater intensity, into the latter with greater variety. They require very detailed study. Their apparent simplicity is deceptive, because of the ease and mastery with which a great artist has produced his effects and because this simplicity is often the ultimate refinement of well-worn poetic devices.

I am concerned in this volume with the *Canterbury Tales*, and not so much with the tales themselves as with the pilgrimage and its relation to them. "Structurally regarded, the stories are merely long speeches expressing, directly or indirectly, the characters of the several

[8] There is an excellent chapter on modern Chaucer critics in P. van D. Shelly's *The Living Chaucer*, Philadelphia, 1940, pp. 18–38. Like others before him, Shelly castigates the dogmatic assertions in Matthew Arnold's Introduction to Ward's "English Poets." The fairies left many good gifts in Matthew's cradle, but not a sense of humor. And his contention that Chaucer has not the "high seriousness" which he considered necessary for a great classic is certainly open to question. Chaucer's gaiety and lightness of touch in the *Tales* must not mislead us.

persons." [9] Chaucer's pilgrimage, as we all know, differs from most "framework" collections not only in the elaboration of the framework itself, but in its close connection with the individual tales. Other medieval writers had been content to let the stories carry the main interest; Chaucer proceeded in very different fashion. Critic after critic has urged that the pilgrimage is the greatest tale of all. The quarrels and badinage on the highroad, the comments and criticisms of various members of the company, the intimate revelation of individual characteristics, and the vivid portraiture of social types—all this we look for elsewhere in the Middle Ages in vain.

Systematic description and discussion of all the tales, in sequence, with reference to Chaucer's literary art, and comparison with his sources, will not be found in the ensuing pages. This has been done by able writers again and again. Its importance and interest should not be minimized. What we do not have at the present time is explanation, in nontechnical language, of certain fundamental difficulties which are likely to lead the modern reader astray. As the title suggests, the object of this book is to make clear the attitude of Chaucer to his narrative work, so far as this can be divined. It is well for the reader to be to some extent his own literary critic, on the basis of his own careful reading of the text. We too often turn to commentaries instead of familiarizing ourselves with the poet's own words.

Chaucer's achievement is all the more remarkable be-

[9] G. L. Kittredge, *Chaucer and His Poetry*, Cambridge, Mass., 1915, p. 155.

cause of the special difficulties which confronted him in the "publication" of so long a work. His readers or listeners were in a very different case from ourselves. We can keep the pilgrimage well in mind, because we can follow it in convenient form, in a single volume. Medieval readers, on the other hand, if they had the collection in its entirety, so far as this goes, were faced with a huge pile of bulky manuscript. Leaves of vellum very quickly pile up. And listeners had quite as much difficulty in keeping the progressive drama of the journey vividly before them. For—and here again there is a contrast to most other framework stories—the pilgrimage is by its very nature not a static affair; it is constantly on the move, and its interest is continually shifting. Even when the poet is describing his characters in the *General Prologue* as gathered in the Tabard Inn, he sees them already on the way to Canterbury; the Miller leading the procession, the Reeve bringing up the rear, the Sea-Captain riding his nag in sailor fashion, and so forth. The man who drew the charming little pictures in the Ellesmere Manuscript put them all on horseback. And there were further difficulties. Chaucer must have realized that his work would often be taken piecemeal. Making favorite extracts from collections was a common procedure. The *Tales* are a mine of varied ores; anyone could find something to his taste. In a day when there was no printing press, and manuscripts had to be laboriously copied out by hand, it was inevitable that special attention should be given to favored portions, and contrasts and echoes in the framework forgotten. These conditions obviously made it difficult for the poet to achieve his purposes in a satisfactory way. But appreciation of those purposes is nonetheless important. Chaucer persisted in his artistic method, even though it was not wholly suited to the conditions of his own day.

Much time has been devoted to tracing the outlines of the design as a whole. Many critics have paraphrased the journey, in the effort to make its events more vivid, and to relate it properly to the accompanying stories. The devices by which it is at once unified and given variety have been carefully analyzed, particularly the Discussion of Marriage. But, in spite of all this, we have been too much concerned with the separate tales. How often have certain ones been published by themselves, torn from their setting, or with some vestiges of the setting clinging to them! The undergraduate who wrote that the *Canterbury Tales* consist of the *Prologue,* the *Knight's Tale,* and the *Nun's Priest's Tale* is not much to be blamed. A selection is defensible for pedagogical purposes, but it gives a false idea of the larger artistic purpose of the whole. This purpose is only to be perceived by having at hand the full text, since the point and humor often depend not only on what has immediately preceded, but on what is to be found much earlier. Moreover, undue attention has been given to those portions which happen to appeal to modern taste. We ought to make a special effort to understand what we like least, to see why it was of interest to Chaucer. We can never really comprehend him if we refuse to focus our attention on those parts of his work which seem to us tedious or otiose or vulgar.

Comprehension of the pilgrimage as a whole and of its dramatic effects has been obscured most of all, I think, by two things: dislike of the "loose" stories, refusal to consider them as worth the same attention as the rest, and indecision as to the sequence in which the tales ought to be read. Each of these points is so important that it must receive separate and detailed consideration.

"A difference of taste in jokes," says George Eliot, "is a great strain on the affections." So it has been with Chaucer; some of his warmest admirers have been repelled by the coarse bits of badinage on the road to Canterbury and by the tales told by the Miller, Reeve, Summoner, Merchant, and Shipman. Belonging with these, in general literary treatment, is the *Friar's Tale,* though this contains nothing which can give offense, and the brief fragment of the *Cook's Tale.* There are more stories of this salty type than of any other, and they are very intimately connected with the roadside drama. All of them, save one, involve quarrel or discussion among the pilgrims. Indecorum begins almost immediately on the journey, with the second tale, it is continued in the third, and would certainly have characterized the unfinished fourth.

The easiest way to deal with this difficulty is that of the celebrated Dr. Bowdler.

> But what old Chaucer's merry page befits,
> The chaster muse of modern days omits.[10]

Excision wrecks the narrative of the pilgrimage, however; the gaps resulting are too great. And the surgical

[10] William Cowper, *Anti-Thelyphthora; a Tale in Verse,* 1781.

method applied to great literature is not as highly esteemed as it once was. Nowadays, when great licence is common in fiction and on the stage, we look at Chaucer's rosier stories with a more indulgent eye. His scenes of unashamed animality are generally accepted as according with the large and tolerant view of life which he showed in his closing years. "Things called indecent or obscene," says Santayana, "are inextricably woven into the texture of human existence; there can be no completely honest comedy without them." [11] The essentially healthy tone of these tales has often been emphasized, and the brilliancy of their narrative and description fully recognized.[12]

On the other hand, many modern critics, some of them distinguished ones, have blamed Chaucer, or made excuses for him. A. W. Pollard, while admitting that the loose tales are told "marvellously well," maintained that "all that can be said for them is that they are told merrily and thoughtlessly, with no lingering over sin for its own sake, and with a general understanding that these things are done in the land of fiction." Legouis, in commenting on the *Miller's Tale,* observed that one has to pardon great writers for such performances—"ce sont choses que Rabelais eût aimé conter et qu'on ne passe plus qu'à lui, et à Chaucer." A. W.

[11] George Santayana, *Soliloquies in England and Later Soliloquies,* New York, 1922, p. 158.

[12] See especially H. S. Canby, "The English Fabliau," PMLA, XXI (1906), 200 ff.; W. M. Hart, "The Reeve's Tale: a Comparative Study of Chaucer's Narrative Art," *ibid.,* XXIII (1908), 1–44; P. van D. Shelly, *The Living Chaucer,* pp. 242 ff.

Ward, in the "English Men of Letters" volume, called the poet's plea that he must tell stories in character and his advice to the reader to turn the page if one of them gives offense, "transparent sophistry," and accused him of "recklessly disregarding bounds the neglect of which was even in his day offensive to many besides the 'precious folk' of whom he half derisively pretends to stand in awe." All that Chesterton could see in the Miller's Tale was "a pail of slops." Miss Chute speaks of the Reeve's "sewer of a mind," and the "cheap jokes which served as [Chaucer's] point of departure." A. A. Jack, professor in the University of Aberdeen, thought that there was the same immoralism in Chaucer as in Fielding.[13]

I do not think that we need linger very long over these comments. How do we know that Chaucer wrote these tales "thoughtlessly"? Even a master cannot produce pieces of so high a degree of finish without reflection and care. Why is it sophistry to advise turning the leaf if the reader is not pleased? May it not be a bit of genial and practical wisdom? As for morals, no one has ever succeeded in setting up a standard for all time, and that of the fourteenth century was certainly very different from our own. We are inclined to look today at objections on this score as relics of Victorian squeam-

[13] A. W. Pollard, Chaucer (a Primer), London, 1895, p. 122. É. Legouis, Geoffroy Chaucer, Paris, 1910, p. 161. A. W. Ward, Chaucer, New York, 1880, p. 181. G. K. Chesterton, Chaucer, New York, 1932, p. 170. Marchette Chute, Geoffrey Chaucer of England, New York, 1946, p. 269. A. A. Jack, A Commentary on the Poetry of Chaucer and Spenser, Glasgow, 1920, p. 99.

ishness. But there is still some feeling, I think, that the rosier tales are not as literature quite deserving of the same attention as the others. The excision of these tales in texts for elementary students, which is certainly wise, has tended to support this. R. K. Root, one of the best of Chaucer scholars, has expressed the view that the poet "deliberately chose to insert the tales [of the Miller and the Reeve], not as works of art, nor even as a necessary part of a great artistic whole, but merely as a diverting interlude." [14] But can we be sure that Chaucer regarded them as less artistic than the more decorous stories? Do not the tales of the Miller and the Reeve, with another from the Cook—unhappily not finished— make a pretty long interlude? Other questions, too, press with insistence for an answer. Why did so wise and tender a poet, Dryden's "perpetual fountain of good sense," descend with apparent relish to the level of yokels and knaves? How did he, a professed aristocratic poet, square himself with an elegant court and fastidious literary friends? There must have been something to apologize for, or he would not have inserted the disclaimers in the *General Prologue* and the *Miller's Prologue,* or have penned the *Retraction.*

I shall not, at the present juncture, endeavor to sum up the discussion of these matters in Chapter III, but one or two points may be made immediately. In the first place, the difficulty in Chaucer's day was clearly one of taste, not of morals. His apologies, particularly

[14] R. K. Root, *The Poetry of Chaucer,* revised ed., Boston, etc., 1922, p. 176.

those in the *Retraction,* have been greatly misunderstood. The more we study the conditions of medieval life, the representation in art of subjects which we consider taboo, and the evidence derived from literature, the plainer this becomes. Nothing, I am sure, would have surprised Chaucer more than the suggestion that any of his tales might corrupt the imagination. We may dismiss immediately the notion that they were in his day considered immoral. But they were most emphatically not good form as coming from a court poet. The fourteenth century was extremely sensitive to decorum, and poets were hedged about by rigid conventions. Comic low-class tales might be all right for minstrels at the cross-roads, and gentlemen and ladies might even condescend to laugh at them, but they were not the proper stuff for an aristocratic versifier. In the *Retraction* we have also to consider the theological idea that a poet should devote his talents to the service of God. I believe that the tales based on fabliau material were just the ones which chiefly interested Chaucer when he began the Canterbury collection; the ones which he most wanted to write; and that he saw, as no one had seen in Britain before his time, the rich possibilities which this type offered for exploitation in English. Furthermore, I believe that absorption in the fabliau and desire to experiment with it were in part the reasons why Chaucer undertook the *Canterbury Tales* and selected a pilgrimage, on which any kind of story might be told, as a setting.

When the detailed evidence presented in Chapter III

volume. But decision between one method of arrangement or the other can be made—and cannot be avoided. For the drama of the pilgrimage obviously depends upon the arrangement of the acts in the drama. We shall find that the whole problem is much simplified if we confine ourselves to questions of sequence and try to determine how far manuscript authority for this is valid, without exploring the exceedingly complicated interrelations of the various manuscripts. Though conclusions as to order are often made to depend on these interrelations, the root of the matter is not reached in such a way. The fundamental question is: shall we feel free to rearrange certain sections of the *Tales,* in order to avoid gross contradictions in the logical order of events on the journey? Or shall we pin our faith to the sequence in the manuscripts, no one of which presents such a logical order of events? The later editions, it will be observed, do not necessarily represent an improvement over the work of the Chaucer Society in this regard, but pursue a different method, which is itself an old one revived.

A review and restatement of this whole problem in clear and simple terms, so far as this can be achieved, will give the layman some idea of the difficulties of the Chaucer editor and critic and the reasons for the procedure in this volume. Perhaps it is not a bad thing for the man who reads for literary enjoyment to have a demonstration of how greatly dependent he really is on "dry" and technical research. Gentle readers who are bored by such matters may, however, omit Chapter IV if they choose. The expert will, I hope, find some interest in a survey of the whole question in its broad outlines. The evidence is now in, and very detailed it is; the time has come for careful decision. I think this decision must be that the best practical solution is to read the *Tales* in the order in the *Oxford Chaucer,* and in accordance with this I have traced the progress of the pilgrimage in Chapter V. Printing the whole in the sequence of any one manuscript does not seem to me advisable, except as a basis for strictly technical work.[15]

After deciding which sequence of tales shall be followed, we may examine the devices by which Chaucer gave his pilgrimage variety, coherence, and dramatic quality. The chief of these devices is the Discussion of Marriage, which I consider in Chapter V.

The greatest dangers in a collection of stories regarded as an art form are monotony and lack of unity. Down through the ages narrators have tried to escape the first of these perils by framing their tales in still another tale, and the second by grouping them about one or more definite themes. Chaucer adopted the first method at the start, and, after the pilgrimage was well under way, the second. The Discussion of Marriage occupies the story-telling at its height, and some of the most brilliant of the tales are only to be understood against this background. The old, old question whether husband or wife shall rule the roost is brought up, debated, and illustrated pro and con in argument and narrative. A hint is dropped; marital and celibate sensibilities are flicked on the raw; strong language alter-

---

[15] For suggestions as to texts and commentaries helpful to the layman, see Appendix.

nates with deadly innuendo. But great care is taken that there shall not be too much of all this. The quarrel dies out, and other interests engage the company—then of a sudden the smoldering spark bursts into flame.

A good deal has been written on this subject, but something more, I think, remains to be said. The Discussion, in any event, offers an excellent basis for consideration of Chaucer's artistic method in developing the pilgrimage. It is not, of course, the only device for unification of effect. The personal quarrels of the Reeve and the Miller, the Summoner and the Friar, and others have to be considered, but these are not so fully exploited and have nothing to do with marriage. And Chaucer "planted" in the *General Prologue* yet another means for sustaining interest: the agreement that the teller of the best tale shall have a supper at the common cost. Who is he? Reader, can you guess? We do not know, alas! And we can only speculate as to how this ticklish business would have been managed.

In Chapter VI we must look with especial care at the ending of the *Tales*. Although his work is unfinished, Chaucer did make an end after a fashion. Annotations and comments on any classic usually flourish much more luxuriantly at the beginning than at the end. The opening lines of the *Iliad* or of *Beowulf* or of *Hamlet* have set many more pens to scratching than those at the close. This is true of the *Canterbury Tales,* and there is a special reason why it should be so. The brilliant descriptions and high spirits of the *General Prologue* and the earlier stories are far more attractive than what we meet in the somewhat inferior *Manciple's Tale,* the Parson's long moralizings, and the gloomy *Retraction* at the end. Yet some very interesting questions present themselves. Why did the poet give up his elaborate scheme for about a hundred and twenty tales, as announced in the *General Prologue,* and make an abrupt and pious ending? Are the stories of the Manciple and Parson to be understood as told on the journey to Canterbury or on the return to London? How are the curious discrepancies in the time of day when these two narratives are told to be explained? How can the indications of place be reconciled with the amount of storytelling on the last day? Is the *Retraction* genuine? If so, does it reflect literary convention or personal conviction? These are perplexing matters, but we need not despair of getting some light on them.

Such, then, is the pleasant program which lies before us in the pages that follow. First of all, however, some discussion of critical principles appears to be in order. This will concern chiefly realism and artifice in the descriptions of the pilgrims and the pilgrimage, with special attention to the social and literary conditions affecting ā fourteenth-century writer. No one can dogmatize as to the right method of approaching Chaucer's work, but anyone can make his choice, state it clearly, and do his best to justify his faith. This I endeavor to do in the chapter which follows, in order that later pages may be encumbered as little as possible by general considerations.

►§II. REALISM AND ARTIFICE

AT THE TIME when he put together the Canterbury collection, Chaucer was in a much more independent position than were most contemporary men of letters.

As we all know, a writer in the later Middle Ages could in most cases reach only a very small circle of readers, since, unlike his modern brother, he was not able to put forth his work in hundreds or thousands of copies, but was restricted to a very limited number of manuscripts, written out in a slow, laborious, and expensive fashion.[1] Furthermore, he had to contend with the strong preference for older work, which had stood the test of time and carried the weight of antiquity. Originality and individuality were only just beginning to prevail over authority; the first gleams of the Renaissance were only just reddening the horizon in England. If a man had something to say, he still endeavored to appear to be passing on the torch. Anonymity, the natural result of deference to tradition, was indeed being to some extent abandoned; writers were beginning to get over the fear of making their work distinctive, of setting it apart as their own. The roll of British "authors" was starting in good earnest with Chaucer, Rolle, Langland, Gower, and Wiclif. But literature in the later fourteenth century may still be conveniently classified by

[1] G. G. Coulton, *Medieval Panorama,* New York and Cambridge, Eng., 1938, p. 538, estimates that in Chaucer's day "it would cost just about as much to get a respectable fair copy of a book made as, in our own, to print an edition of 500 copies."

types. Writing as a profession, as we understand it, did not exist. No man could unaided make a living by his pen. Everyone was dependent upon patronage, either of the Church or of some wealthy or noble personage. This implied no loss of dignity; the man of letters had much to give in return for what he received. But unless he had very remarkable ability his influence did not extend far beyond the immediate circle of court or cloister.

Chaucer's dependence was, of course, upon lay patronage; the earlier part of his life, when he was obviously a gifted and popular young man, composing "balades, roundels, virelayes" in the French style, and longer pieces sometimes designed as courtly compliments, illustrates this well enough. His alliance, through his wife, with the family of John of Gaunt, was sufficient to make any poet's fortune. As time went on, and he proved himself exceedingly able in business and diplomacy, he was probably regarded as quite as distinguished in public affairs as in poetry. His long service in the Customs has been compared to that of Charles Lamb in the India House, but Lamb was a clerk doing a routine duty, while Chaucer had the supervision of one of the chief sources of the royal revenue, at a time when funds were badly needed and honest collectors essential. The fact that he was for a long time obliged to write out the rolls in his own hand does not mean that he was only a hireling, but that the bookkeeping had to be done by someone who could be trusted. The extraordinary thing is that despite all this labor he was able to devote himself to writing poetry. And the longer he worked at his official duties, the more brilliant his poetry became.

In 1386 he gave up his place in the customhouse. It used to be thought that this was not voluntary, but there are convincing reasons for believing that he was anxious to retire and enjoy some well-earned leisure, in which he could devote himself to literary work.[2] He had twice obtained permission to employ a deputy, and in 1385 he asked to have this made permanent. Very likely several causes led to his retirement. His very desirable Aldgate residence had perhaps been obtained through court favor, and he may have lost it in the shifting sunshine of such favor.[3] It is generally supposed that the year 1387 marks the beginning of his work in assembling the *Tales* and writing the *General Prologue,* though there are other views, and the fixing of a definite year can be only a guess. But in any case he had by 1387 been made a justice of the peace in Kent, taken his place in Parliament as a Knight of the Shire, given up his residence in London, and gone to live in the country.

[2] J. M. Manly, *Canterbury Tales,* New York, 1928, p. 18 f.

[3] Haldeen Braddy gives evidence to show that Chaucer and his wife were well acquainted with Alice Perrers, the influential mistress of Edward III; that especially as an Aldgate landowner she may have assisted in the granting of a free lease to Chaucer's house, and as a power at court in the bestowal of the Comptrollership of Customs upon him. "Her loss of influence after the decease of her husband would, in turn, best explain Chaucer's surrender in 1386 of the deed to Aldgate and the end of his Comptrollership." ("Chaucer and Dame Alice Perrers," *Speculum,* XXI [1946], 222–228.) Even if all these surmises are not true, Dame Alice is a lady who deserves attention.

His reputation as a writer was now great; it was not confined to the court and the literary men in London, but extended through the country wherever reading was done, and also across the Channel. Notices in the fourteenth century are few, but just when Chaucer is usually held to have begun the *Tales* Thomas Usk wrote in the *Testament of Love:* "In goodnes of gentyl man-lyche speche without any maner of nycite [folly] of storieres ymagynacion in wytte and in good reason of sentence he passeth al other makers." John Gower, in the first version of the *Confessio Amantis* (1390), made Venus say:

> Of Ditees and of Songes glade,
> The whiche he for mi sake made,
> The lond fulfild is oueral.

There is the best of testimony to his fame in France. The bitter and jealous Eustache Deschamps, "poète officiel de la France," as Petit de Julleville calls him, addressed to Chaucer a *balade* of the highest praise, comparing him to Socrates, Seneca, and Ovid, which is doubly significant, since Deschamps hated the English. His many rewards and perquisites, of which we are fortunate to have records, may have been bestowed upon him chiefly for public services, but that he deserved recompense as a poet cannot have been forgotten. In 1399, when he appealed for money to the new sovereign, Henry IV, he did so, not in a businesslike prose communication, but in a rhymed *compleynt.* The evidences of his fame in the fifteenth century and the large number of manuscripts of his works are not without significance for the closing years of his life. Particularly interesting are the tributes by Lydgate, Hoccleve, James I of Scotland, and others.[4]

At the time of his retirement to Kent, then, he was in a position to write for his own satisfaction in the ambitious work which he was just beginning. He was not endeavoring to please a patron, as in the *Book of the Duchesse,* or celebrating a royal marriage, as in the *Parliament of Birds,* or starting out to give a great piece of court news an allegorical setting, as in the *House of Fame.*[5] He was not submitting his work to the correction of literary friends, as in the *Troilus.* In many of his early poems he had given rein to his own individuality, and still more in the *Troilus* and the prologue to the *Legend of Good Women;* now he felt free to do this as never before. On the pilgrimage to Canterbury he not only introduces himself in person—one of the commonest devices of the medieval storyteller—but gives himself an important part in the action and makes himself constantly felt, not as a narrator, but as Geoffrey Chaucer in person. When he breaks in with his own reflections, he does not destroy the illusion, as Thackeray

[4] For the quotations in this paragraph see Miss C. F. E. Spurgeon's *Five Hundred Years of Chaucer Criticism and Allusion,* I, 8, 10.

[5] Of course we do not know how he intended to finish this poem, since it is incomplete, but why a journey to the houses of Fame and Rumor, unless tidings of some great event were to follow? It looks as if he found it inexpedient to reveal these tidings—court poets have to be wary—but decided to let the account of his marvellous journey stand for its own sake. Possibly the *Parliament* has no personal application.

does in *Vanity Fair,* by telling us that the personages are only puppets in a box. Though in a famous passage he is described by the Host as abstracted and "elvish," he quickly establishes a confidential relation with his fellow pilgrims ("so hadde I spoken with hem everichon"), and not less so with his reader, treating him like a dear and intimate friend, from whom he will keep no secrets and whom he will never willingly deceive—though alas! he does deceive him constantly, as we shall see. There is nothing to match this in the Middle Ages, early or late.

It is a familiar generalization that medieval narrative is seldom realistic, that writers were little concerned to set down what they saw with their own eyes, but rather what was proper, according to convention, that they should see. This was, of course, partly the result of that submergence of the author in the stream of tradition which has just been emphasized. Storytellers were less interested in description and characterization than in action and sentiment, and description and characterization, when they did appear, were likely to run into welltried molds. If life is conceived as an allegory, or as a game played according to courtly rules, or as an illustration of religious formulas, the actors are likely to become conventionalized too. Celtic story, so potent in imagination, had emphasized the remote, the fanciful, and the supernatural. To this French artistry had added schematization and self-consciousness. The merry rhymed tales of the jongleurs, the folk tales and traditional ballads, were in description poor and conventional. The saga writers in Iceland, still continuing their work in Chaucer's day, had developed a superb and simple narrative prose, but they relied for their effects on narrative and dialogue, generally leaving character to be inferred.

One of the most astonishing things about the *Canterbury Tales* is that Chaucer, a courtly artist, steeped in French, Latin, and Italian models, chose as a framework a direct departure from them. He did not have to go to sleep and dream in order to get started, or bother any longer about personified abstractions and the conventions of courtly love. A pilgrimage was one of the commonest sights in fourteenth-century England. Canterbury was, of course, not the only goal; there were great shrines to be visited to the west, in Salisbury, Bath, and Glastonbury—where the monks had a complete set of St. Dunstan's bones "in rivalry to the set at Canterbury." [6] Chaucer aimed to give the illusion, not of an imaginary world, but of the real one, and the more real the world of his setting, the more his tales would by contrast seem like tales, even though some of them might deal with everyday life in realistic fashion. But this is not to say that he thought realism better than convention, or that he was ready to throw convention overboard. Artificial forms and concepts are, of course, very common in the tales themselves, though it is clear that his attitude toward them had in some measure changed. We get a strong hint of this from the *Legend of Good*

[6] G. M. Trevelyan, *England in the Age of Wycliffe,* London, 1899, p. 340.

Women, begun, apparently, just before he devoted his major energies to the Canterbury collection, and revised about 1394, after that collection was well under way. The *Prologue* embodies the good old stuff—the dream-opening, the God of Love and his Queen, the poet as sinner and the penance imposed upon him. This was the sort of thing that the English court expected of its poets; though the old machinery creaked a bit, it was still running. Chaucer exploited the decorative qualities of such poetry to the full, but he no longer took it quite seriously. Ostensibly, the *Legend* is an expression of regret for his sin in having slandered women in the *Troilus,* and a making of amends by celebrating female martyrs for love. He kept the *Prologue* in the conventional pattern, but when he got to the legends he could not quite keep his tongue out of his cheek. Thus, after celebrating the "martyr" Cleopatra, he adds:

> Now, or I fynde a man thus trewe and stable,
> And wol for love his deth so frely take,
> I preye God let oure hedes nevere ake! Amen.

In the story of Lucrece he says that Christ tells us that nowhere in Israel did he find such faith as in a woman; this is no lie, but look at the tyranny of men—the truest of them cannot be trusted! Such waggishness as this must have pained his good friend Gower, inching along with deadly seriousness on his vast *Confessio Amantis.* That Chaucer intended the *Legend* as a travesty,[7] is,

[7] This theory was vigorously, if somewhat hastily, developed by H. C. Goddard, "Chaucer's Legend of Good Women," JEGP, VII

however, generally considered a mistake. In the midst of a court still devoted to the traditions of the past, he was assuredly not attacking romantic conventions. But he had reached a point where he could afford to have a little quiet fun with them. In similar fashion he put into the *Knight's Tale,* a revision of an earlier *Palamon and Arcite,* some remarks not at all in keeping with its general tone. At the same time, he clearly recognized the artistic possibilities of the metrical romance, and thought highly of it, otherwise he would not have given the *Knight's Tale* the place of honor in the pilgrimage.

Most medieval frameworks enshrining collections of tales were frankly artificial, but experiments had already been made with realism. The most famous is, of course, the *Decameron* of Boccaccio. To the old question whether it influenced Chaucer only an indecisive answer can be given.[8] No one of the *Tales* is necessarily dependent upon it, and the general plan of the enveloping action is very different. We wonder why Chaucer, with his intimate knowledge of so much of Boccaccio's other work, does not show unmistakable acquaintance with

---

(1908), 87–129; VIII (1909), 47–111. In the latter volume J. L. Lowes presented an elaborate rebuttal: "Is Chaucer's *Legend of Good Women* a Travesty?" pp. 513–569. There is a brief, but suggestive, article by R. M. Garrett, " 'Cleopatra the Martyr' and Her Sisters," JEGP, XXII (1923), 64–74. There seems little doubt that Lowes was right in his main contention, but I agree with Garrett that he "allows too little for Chaucer's originality or for his spirit of fun" (p. 67, note 8). Conventional elements should not be overemphasized.

[8] For an admirable discussion of this, see Bryan and Dempster, *Sources and Analogues of Chaucer's Canterbury Tales,* Chicago, 1941, pp. 13 ff. (Pratt and Young).

the *Decameron,* but it does not seem to have been current in either France or England in his day. No French translation is known until after his death, and the earliest English version is still later.[9] Chaucer may possibly have known some part of it at first hand, or have heard of its general plan. But we can only conjecture. The point for us to consider here is, not that he far excelled the Italian master in artistry, but—something not generally observed—that he held consistently to realism, whereas Boccaccio quickly slipped back into frank artificiality.

The description of the great plague of 1348, with which the *Decameron* begins, is not less vivid than the pages of Defoe. It is professedly of an eye-witness, with striking touches; he himself, says Boccaccio, observed that two hogs, rooting among the clothes of a corpse, were straightway stricken, and fell dead, as if by poison. But when he begins his narrative proper, with the meeting of seven young ladies in the church of Santa Maria Novella in Florence, he reports it as from "a trustworthy person"—an old trick of the storyteller. This group is increased to ten, a convenient round number, by the arrival of three young gentlemen. A luxurious country house is a fit setting for their elegant diversions. The longer the narrative continues, the more formal and artificial do these diversions appear, with the division of the stories into groups of ten for ten days, the arrangement of these for each day (save two only) about a set

[9] W. E. Farnham, "England's Discovery of the 'Decameron,'" PMLA, XXXIX (1924), 123–139.

theme, the election of a sovereign to preside, and the formality of the entertainment in the evening, which follows quite a regular pattern—music, a dance, and an artistically composed song. All this is almost as stylized as a medieval tapestry, and is in striking contrast to the sustained realism of Chaucer's journey, with its quarrels, discussions, and rude interruptions. There is, indeed, a little variety now and then in Boccaccio's narrative: the company moves to another country-seat, the scenic beauty of which is stressed, and on one occasion a lively quarrel breaks out between two servants. But in general there is little realism. The different members of the group, who are all of the same social station, are little individualized. Attempts to distinguish them by their chance remarks or by etymologies of their names are fruitless. The only one who stands out with any clearness is Dioneo, a Mercutio who mingles smut and gaiety. Consequently there is none of the careful fitting of story to teller generally observable in the Canterbury collection. The exchanges of opinion are usually tame and conventional. Except for the proem, introduction and epilogue, Boccaccio only once speaks out. The stories are of various kinds. Realistic and racy anecdotes in an artificial setting produce an effect which is not altogether happy. Chaucer never managed things thus.

The case was very different with Giovanni Sercambi, a mediocre literary figure who has achieved a belated renown through the possibility that his work influenced Chaucer. He was no court poet, burning, like Boccaccio, to charm a fair lady, but a solid citizen of Lucca, the son

of an apothecary, a dealer in books and writing ma-
terials, who had gained some prominence in soldiering
and public affairs. In his leisure moments he grasped the
pen, and among other undertakings produced his imitation of the *Decameron.* He had little originality. His
collection of tales starts, like Boccaccio's, with a group
gathered in a church, planning to escape the Black
Death. The general plan of what follows is suggested
by one Aluisi, who, like Pampinea in Florence, is elected
to make arrangements for the diversion of the party.
Sercambi himself is chosen as teller of the tales.

It must not be forgotten that Sercambi's collection is
extant only in a later and enlarged form, which cannot
have been completed before 1385; an earlier version, the
so-called *Novelliero,* conjecturally dated 1374, is now
lost, but we have evidence that it contained a hundred
tales divided into ten days, with a song and other amusements at the end of each day. So when we consider
the possible influence of Sercambi on the *Canterbury
Tales,* we ought to remember that if it exists it probably came from the *Novelliero,* not from the later
novelle. In the latter Sercambi enlarged his original,
breaking the earlier mold, in order to get in more tales—
one hundred and fifty-five in the extant manuscript.

The resemblances and differences between Sercambi
and Chaucer may be studied at the reader's leisure.
That there is any real indebtedness seems very doubtful.
Both expeditions do, indeed, consist of a large and varied
company of men and women, constantly on the move,
and the author is one of the party. But Sercambi's jour-

ney is not a religious affair, and the tales are not told by different members of the group. Many details which have been cited as common to both collections are insignificant, or such as might naturally arise from the general situation. There is little real resemblance in the incidental amusements, and the differentiation of some of Sercambi's stories in order to apply to certain groups in his company is not at all like Chaucer's method.[10]

[10] I must differ from some of the conclusions in the excellent discussion by Pratt and Young, in Bryan and Dempster's *Sources and Analogues,* to which I am indebted. Comparison of the *Canterbury Tales* with other framework stories would lead us too far afield. A review of the latter, with full bibliography, is given in Bryan and Dempster, pp. 1 ff. Not quite enough attention is usually given to Robert Mannyng of Brunne's *Handlyng Synne* (1303), in which the tales are arranged on the basis of the Seven Deadly Sins, the Ten Commandments, and the Seven Sacraments. Robert, a Lincolnshire monk, based his work on a mediocre French manual written by a Yorkshire cleric in the reign of Edward I. But the stories, many of which are due to Robert himself and not to his source, are remarkable for their picturesqueness, their keen observation of English manners and customs, their attacks on sinful pleasures such as dancing and tournaments, and their satire of current social life.

The contrast between formalism and realism may be illustrated by two fourteenth-century Spanish collections. There is no evidence that Chaucer was acquainted with them, and every probability that he was not. *El Conde Lucanor* (1328–1335) by Don Juan Manuel, is a series of short vernacular tales in a framework, with a strong didactic flavor. The setting is very stiff and very simple, and follows a similar pattern for each tale. The *libro de buen amor,* by Juan Ruiz, Archpriest of Hita, a small town near Guadalajara, affords a sharp contrast. The Archpriest, a contemporary of Don Juan Manuel, produced a picaresque autobiography, the formlessness of which, with vivid pictures of contemporary life, gives the effect of realism. The inserted narratives were drawn from Latin sources, from fabliaux, from Eastern and Western apologues, from romances, etc. Fitz-Maurice

That the *Canterbury Tales* show far greater variety and subtlety of effect than the *Decameron* is no reproach to Boccaccio. We say that the *Knight's Tale* represents an advance over the *Teseide,* and the *Troilus* over the *Filostrato,* but the Italian sources are fine poems. In these and in the *Decameron* Boccaccio accomplished what he set out to do, and accomplished it brilliantly. But in the *Tales* Chaucer achieved greater interest through dramatic treatment, closer organic union between setting and stories, and greater contrast in the stories themselves as highly individualized narratives told by persons of different social station. By such means he avoided one of the greatest weaknesses of the narrative prose and verse of his own day—monotony. In the Middle Ages there was commonly little variation of mood and expression in one and the same work; the note struck at the outset was maintained to the end. Changes might be rung on the main theme, but this

---

Kelly says: "Like Chaucer, Ruiz had an almost incomparable gust for life, an immitigable gaiety of spirit, which penetrates his transcription of the Human Comedy. Like Chaucer, his adventurous curiosity led him to burst the bonds of the prison-house, and to confer upon his country new rhythms and metres." But he was far less of an artist. Moreover, Chaucer, in spite of his love for depicting rascals, always preserved a cool ironic detachment. The Archpriest was a rascal, not a gentleman.

For Don Juan Manuel see the edition by Eduardo Juliá, *Serie escogida de autores espagnoles,* Madrid, 1933, and the translation by James York, *Count Lucanor, or the Fifty Pleasant Stories of Patronio,* London, 1868, 1899, 1924 (with new introduction). For the Archpriest, the edition by J. Cajador, *Clásicos castellaños,* XIV, XVII, Madrid, 1913. The quotation from Fitz-Maurice Kelly will be found in his *History of Spanish Literature,* New York, 1900, p. 79.

theme continued to beat upon the ear. The charm of contrast was little recognized. Literary form was likely to remain unvaried; romances ran on for thousands of lines in rhymed octosyllabics, and *chansons de geste* in unrelieved blocks of assonance. So with mood; life was either to be enjoyed by the light-hearted or reformed with the moralists. Laughter and tears, the comic and the tragic, so constantly blended in this world, almost never found expression together. It is one of the marks of Chaucer's greatness that he achieved this, and with surpassing ease and grace, making his storytelling seem like a veracious picture of real life. His pilgrimage is as remote from our own experience as are the tavern scenes in *Henry IV,* but we feel, just as we do in the company of Falstaff and his crew, that this is what we might see could we by some magic turn the clock back a few centuries.

There is really no necessity to search for the "source" of Chaucer's pilgrimage. It would, indeed, have been strange had there been no reflections in imaginative literature of the common medieval custom of going on a journey with a party of travelers. In days when roads were bad, lodgings dubious, and thieves abundant, such a party was safest. Mutual protection and assistance were clearly in the interest of all. And this was one of the few ways of escaping from humdrum everyday life and seeing something of the world. The rise of the middle class had brought increased congestion in cities and towns, under living conditions which we should think intolerable in crowding, lack of sanitation, and absence of personal privacy. If one went on a pilgrimage to the shrine of a saint, he had the double satisfaction of piety and diversion. Good business was enjoyed by those who had lodgings for travelers along the way, particularly by religious houses, where a donation to the local saint might be expected. Many guidebooks were written, sometimes disguised as fiction, the importance of which for literature has only recently been recognized. Thus, the celebrated "travels" of the fictitious Sir John Mandeville were based on medieval Baedekers, and Bédier has shown that the *chansons de geste,* which used to be thought heroic epic stuff based on earlier lays, were mainly due to the collaboration of monks and minstrels advertising local saints and heroes in order to induce a stay at hostels where their memory was venerated. Pious donors often financed pilgrims: in 1361 a vintner left twenty shillings to anyone willing to walk to Canterbury "with naked feet," forty shillings to one going to St. Mary of Walsingham.[11] Those who traveled with a company had the solace of entertainments at night and at stopping-places. The jollifications on pilgrimages, indeed, grew to scandalous excesses, and were vigorously attacked by satirists and churchmen. But perhaps these excesses have been exaggerated today. In any case, storytelling, one of the commonest forms of medieval entertainment in a crowd, was probably frequent. The very fact that Chaucer, Sercambi, and

[11] E. P. Kuhl, "Chaucer's Burgesses," *Transactions of the Wisconsin Academy of Sciences, Arts and Letters,* XVIII (Part 2, 1916), 652–675; see esp. p. 675. There is much interesting material in this essay.

others [12] make their travelers turn to it for relaxation is significant.

The realism of the pilgrimage is, of course, in large measure due to personal observation. Chaucer had seen much of the world, and he was now to a greater degree than ever looking at it through his own eyes. When he tells us that he is reporting what he saw we should often believe him.

> I seigh his sleves purfiled at the hond
> With grys, and that the fyneste of a lond.

> A clote-leef he hadde under his hood
> For swoot, and for to keep his heed from heete.
> But it was joye for to seen hym swete!

Attention is naturally devoted to the pilgrims rather than to localities or scenery. Nobody needed to be told how the road from London to Canterbury looked, or what sort of place the Tabard Inn was. Such matters were familiar. The travelers fill the canvas; it is to them, their appearance, conversation, and narratives that our attention is directed.

It has sometimes been conjectured that Chaucer was in the main describing an actual pilgrimage to Canter-

---

[12] Erasmus, in the preface to his *Praise of Folly,* says that, recently journeying from Italy to England, he did not want to waste all the hours on horseback "in idle talk and popular stories." In the *Dialogus miraculorum* of Caesar of Heisterbach, a cardinal, the most distinguished man in the company, calls out: "Quis vestrum dicet nobis aliquid boni?" An anecdote is then told, "ad quod verbum Cardinalis subridens, sermonem commendavit." Beatrice D. Brown, "A Thirteenth-century Chaucerian Analogue," MLN, LII (1937), 28–31. These are straws that show the direction of the wind.

bury of which he was a member, or that the stages of the journey and the stopping places can be determined accurately, or that the descriptions of some of the company were so faithful that the originals could have been recognized.

Before we consider the details of such theories, it may be well to recall that the *Canterbury Tales* is a work of art and that its realism must not deceive us into forgetting its artificial elements. The more closely we examine it, the more clearly we can see that much is in direct contradiction to actual fact. Realism is not reality; it is a collective term for the devices that give the effect of reality. In painting, green pigment makes a sky look blue; in architecture, a curve sometimes gives the impression of a straight line. So poetry, even when dealing with everyday life, must modify, suppress, emphasize, exaggerate, and invent. This is a very elementary point, but it is extraordinary how often it is overlooked. Like Joe Bagstock, Chaucer is "dev'lish sly." He deceives you—as he should—with the most innocent air in the world. The pilgrimage conveys so convincingly the illusion of reality that its artifices have often been forgotten and its conventions neglected. They begin, indeed, with the very first lines of the *General Prologue,* "Whan that Aprille with his shoures soote," etc., which seemed to Lowell "a breath of uncontaminate springtide," lifting the hair on his forehead. But Lowell did not know or remember that the springtime opening was a hackneyed device.[13] Chaucer gave it the right touch to

[13] Rosemond Tuve, *Seasons and Months,* Paris, 1933, and references by Tatlock, MLN, LI (1936), 280, note 6.

make its artificialities vanish. More than this, he constantly persuades us to accept conventions which directly contradict reality. It is a convention that some thirty people, strung out on horseback along a muddy road, can hear the voice of one narrator. It is a convention that such a company, gathered by chance, should all be expert storytellers; that a drunken miller can tell a tale full of brilliant characterization and nicely balanced action, or a bluff soldier like the Knight weave a romance with all the art of a seasoned minstrel. It is a convention that the poet can reproduce the exact words of long stories. It is a convention that two of the company repeat as tales long prose treatises, smelling strongly of the lamp and stuffed with learned citations. It is a convention that everyone, with these exceptions, speaks in rhymed verse. And so one might continue. Such violations of literal truth, however, win ready acquiescence. The art of the stage makes similar demands: the "aside," not supposed to be heard by the actors, is audible to the gallery gods; the soliloquy brings the most secret thoughts into the open. In opera, everybody sings. Those who have seen *The Yellow Jacket,* a Chinese drama in English dress, will recall how quickly the drab and ubiquitous property man, moving about among the brilliantly costumed actors, is forgotten, and how the baldest devices pass muster—a block of wood doing duty for a baby, a heap of tables for a barge floating down a stream. Conversely, absolute realism on the stage is usually ineffective; real water or real trees are inferior to imitations of gauze and lath. When we see such ultra-realistic pieces as *Ghosts* or *The Cherry Orchard,* we feel as if we were witnessing actual events, unmodified by art. Nothing could be farther from the truth; they are full of the devices of the theater.

These considerations may seem very obvious. But critics who would unhesitatingly agree to them are sometimes led to ignore them and take Chaucer's statements at their face value in the effort to penetrate into his plans and intentions. For example, there has been much discussion as to how many days he meant us to assume that his pilgrimage covered on the way to Canterbury. Study of court records points now to two days, now to three, now to four. Convenient resting places were Dartford (fifteen miles); Rochester (another fifteen); Ospringe (sixteen more); which leaves ten miles to Canterbury. But attempts to make any set scheme square satisfactorily with the storytelling and what we are told of the journey appear fruitless. Definiteness is lacking. We are not told where the pilgrims stopped for the night. It would have been impossible to get sixty tales, of the average caliber of those we have, told between London and Canterbury, with the intervening discussions, even in four days. The tale of the Knight would consume at least a morning. The conclusion is that accuracy and consistency in the details of the journey must not be expected and that this does not matter. Readers and listeners are not like scholars, bothered if things do not work out precisely; what they are after is the story. Inconsistencies must not be too glaring, however; and it is probably for this reason that Chaucer left the stages of his journey vague. Dante was cautious in narrating his progress through the Inferno. "The journey through Hell being physically impossible, Dante purposely refrains from furnishing particulars that might destroy the illusion." [14]

The same principle applies to the question whether Chaucer tried to keep the exact number of pilgrims mentioned at the beginning of the *General Prologue*— nine and twenty. The answer clearly seems to be that he did not bother to be consistent. His first statement is very definite. While he was lodged at the Tabard,

> At nyght was come into that hostelrye
> Wel nyne and twenty in a compaignye,
> Of sondry folk, by aventure yfalle
> In felaweshipe, and pilgrims were they alle,
> That toward Caunterbury wolden ryde.

"Wel" nine and twenty means "no less than" that number. As Miss Hammond long ago pointed out, the nine and twenty plus Chaucer is much like the nineteen ladies plus Alcestis in the prologue to the *Legend of Good Women*.[15] But when we come to reckon up the number of pilgrims later mentioned and described in the *Prologue*, there are thirty, not twenty-nine.[16] Obviously we

[14] *La Divina Commedia,* ed. by C. H. Grandgent, Boston, etc., 1933, p. 46. See Tatlock, "The Duration of the Canterbury Pilgrimage," PMLA, XXI (1906), 478–485; Manly and Rickert, *Text of the Canterbury Tales,* II, 492 ff. Other discussions may be found in the bibliographies.

[15] E. P. Hammond, *Chaucer; a Bibliographical Manual,* New York, 1908, p. 255.   [16] See the list below, p. 56.

must exclude Chaucer himself, who tells us that he had spoken with "hem everichon" and that he proposes to tell us about each "of hem." The Host must also be omitted, since he is not one of those "come into that hostelrye" at night, as must also the Canon and the Canon's Yeoman, who meet the party later on the road. There is to my mind little justification for doubting that the Prioress had three priests with her, and for conjecturing that "and preestes thre" was added by someone else than Chaucer.[17] All the manuscripts have the three priests. It would not be "quite absurd" for two priests besides her confessor to travel with the Prioress; it may be a touch indicating that she was a great lady, or others from her abbey may have joined the pilgrimage. An abbey might have several chaplains. Later on, after the journey is well under way, the Host calls on *the* Nun's Priest for a tale (B 3999). This is best explained as forgetfulness on Chaucer's part, that he did not remember, after a considerable lapse of time, that he had given the Prioress three priests.

It has been ingeniously argued by a distinguished scholar that "Chaucer's description of the Squire in the *Prologue* was not written at the same time as his sketch of the other members of the Canterbury company, but was composed later and inserted in its present position

[17] "Chaucer says in l. 24 that there were nine and twenty pilgrims assembled at the Tabard, and this is exactly accurate if only one priest is counted." (Manly ed., 1928, p. 508.) Robinson (p. 756) followed Manly's lead. But if the three priests are reduced to one there will be 28 pilgrims, not 29.

between the Knight and the Yeman." [18] We are told that it is odd that the Squire's military excursions are dissociated from those of his father; that the Knight ought to have a servant along to groom his horses; that the gay young Squire would hardly have gone on a pilgrimage with only one servant. If we assume that putting him in was an afterthought, we get just twenty-nine pilgrims, as in Chaucer's statement in the *Prologue*.

The important point here is not so much whether the Squire was inserted later as whether the critical method is sound. Ought not artistic effect to be considered quite as much as realistic detail? May not the Knight have been designedly given expeditions fitting an old and seasoned warrior, and the Squire such as might well be undertaken by a lad just winning his spurs? Of course young men often took service outside their own families. Why must we be told how the horses were cared for? This is important in real life, but not in poetry. And may there not be an intentional contrast between the elegance of the young dandy and his deliberate renunciation of some of this elegance on pilgrimage by having only one servant along ("hym liste ride so")?

The late Professor Manly suggested that certain of the pilgrims were drawn from life, that their portraits are those of actual persons, and that these portraits were

[18] Carleton Brown, "The Squire and the Number of the Canterbury Pilgrims," MLN, XLIX (1934), 216–222. I am indebted in various ways to this essay, which deserves careful attention.

recognizable to Chaucer's contemporaries. This theory requires careful scrutiny. Doubts as to its validity have been expressed by others, but so far as I am aware dissent has not gone much beyond expressions of opinion.

In one instance identification of a pilgrim is beyond doubt. The Host is no imaginary figure. His name is given in the prologue to the *Cook's Tale* as "Herry Bailly" (A 4358). In the Subsidy Rolls for Southwark for 1380–81 (4 Richard II) appear "Henri Bayliff Ostyler" and "Christian uxor eius." [19] We are not so fortunate in being sure of the name of the shrewish wife whose tantrums the host describes ($B^2$3079 ff.). It has been argued that "goode lief" ($B^2$3084) is really a proper name, "Goodelief," [20] and it is so printed in the editions

[19] The entry in the Rolls is not always given in the same form. See Skeat, *Oxford Chaucer*, V, 129; Robinson, p. 770. I follow Robinson.

[20] This was proposed by the late Edith Rickert, one of the ablest Chaucer scholars of our time, MP, XXV (1927), 79–82. She noted various occurrences of *"Godlef* or *Godelef,* Latinized as *Godeleva* (once *Godeliva*)" in the Feet of Fines for Kent and the Lewisham Court Rolls. *Godelief* or *Goodelief* seems not to have been found. Eleven MSS write what she considered the proper name as one word, and two of these have *Goodleef* with a capital G. She frankly admitted that "goode lief" (D 431) applied to her fourth husband by the Wife of Bath—

Thanne wolde I seye, "Goode lief, taak keep
How mekely looketh Wilkyn, oure sheep!"

"makes it uncertain whether or not Chaucer intended to use the name [*Goodelief*] when the Host was speaking." This seems a very fair statement of the case. I cannot agree with Miss Rickert that "a proper name in line 3084 gives a better reading," or is "much less awkward." Cf. "that swete wif," "that swete wyght," *Book of the Duchesse*, 1037, 1176. There may well be a designed contrast between the phrase of endearment, "that dear good creature," and the Host's of Manly and Robinson. But that the termagant was named "Goodelief" is by no means certain.

In his entertaining volume *Some New Light on Chaucer,*[21] Professor Manly has given us some very definite statements.

Scholars . . . have taught us that the pilgrimage was purely imaginary and that the group of pilgrims was artificially constructed by Chaucer to include and exhibit representatives of all the principal classes of society and occupational types of his day. . . . perhaps Chaucer's personal interests and prejudices [formed the basis of his choice]. Investigation indicates that some at least of the pilgrims were real persons, and persons with whom Chaucer can be shown to have had definite personal contacts. . . . Allusions which to us mean little or nothing were instantly intelligible to the hearers and readers for whom he wrote. . . . The nobility and gentry numbered not more than a few hundred, and their social life centered in London . . . we may be sure that they caught every sly reference to persons and things they knew. We can understand the spirit and guess at the success of many of

---

gloomy recollections of her rampings. On the other hand, it seems to me no serious objection to Miss Rickert's theory that the name of the wife in the Subsidy Rolls is "Christian." Chaucer may not have known what her real name was, or may have substituted "Goodelief" as a touch of irony, or Harry Bailly may have been more than once married. Perhaps he first wrote "goode lief," and this was later mistaken by scribes for a proper name, or the reverse may have happened. It seems far better to leave the question as Miss Rickert left it in her modest and pleasant article than to regard it as "settled." (Manly, *Some New Light* [see note following], p. 81)

[21] New York, 1926; a revision of the Lowell lectures delivered in Boston in 1924. The extracts will be found on pp. 70–76. They are quoted with the kind permission of Messrs. Henry Holt and Co.

Chaucer's sly "digs" and "hits" only if we think of his work as conceived and received like a local Christmas revue or revel that banters and satirizes persons and incidents familiar to every member of the audience. Chaucer was not writing for posterity or even for the whole contemporary population of England, but for a handful of courtiers, gentlemen, churchmen, professional men, officials, and city merchants.

I do not think that the best scholars have taught us that the pilgrims "include and exhibit representatives of all the principal classes of society and occupational types." It does not need much knowledge of fourteenth-century England to reveal that a great many have been omitted, as Manly urged, and Chaucer himself says that the company gathered in the Tabard Inn were sundry folk, met by chance in fellowship. But it is not a necessary conclusion that the selection was made on the basis of his "personal interests and prejudices." Why not on the basis of his desires as an artist, to exhibit varied and picturesque types, suitable for the telling of his tales? And I do not see how we can be sure that he was writing only for a small group in London. Earlier in this chapter the extent of his contemporary reputation has been emphasized. The care and finish of much of his work in the *Tales* and its occasional deep seriousness and psychological complexity certainly suggest that he had a different aim from tickling with local hits the risibilities of a handful of people. Even granting that he had no thought for posterity or a wider audience, would the nobility and gentry have recognized obscure fellows like the Reeve or the Miller or the Summoner and their ilk, or have been greatly interested if they did? Was Chaucer the kind of man to draw malicious portraits under a thin disguise? Is it not more likely that he took what he needed from actual observation, without intending that his people should be recognizable?

We come back to the point which has already been urged: these *seem* to be portraits, but actually are not. Chaucer may have seen a miller with a wart on his nose or a cook with a sore on his shin, but that does not mean that the whole description is that of a real person. We are told that the Miller's wife is "certainly no artificially constructed type, but a living and highly individualized person." [22] Why must this be so? Was not Chaucer a great enough artist to produce this effect? Read Defoe's vivid fictional portraits, or observe how the *Spectator* did the trick.

The first of our society is a gentleman of Worcestershire, of ancient descent, a baronet, his name Sir Roger de Coverley. . . . When he is in town he lives in Soho Square. It is said he keeps himself a bachelor by reason he was crossed in love by a perverse beautiful widow of the next county to him. . . . He continues to wear a coat and doublet of the same cut that were in fashion at the time of his repulse, which, in his merry humours, he tells us, has been in and out twelve times since he first wore it. He is now in his fifty-sixth year, cheerful, gay, and hearty; keeps a good house both in town and country; a great lover of mankind; but there is such a mirthful cast in his behaviour, that he is rather beloved than esteemed. . . . I must not omit that Sir Roger is a justice of

[22] *Op. cit.,* p. 99.

the quorum; that he fills the chair at a quarter-session with great abilities; and, three months ago, gained universal applause by explaining a passage in the Game Act.

Compare this with the description of the Reeve, one of those which best fits Manly's theory. Here are similar elements—name, personal appearance, place of residence, specific activities, character. The reader may compare with other pilgrims Sir Andrew Freeport and the Templar and Captain Sentry and Will Wimble.

In his edition of the *Tales* (1928) Professor Manly later wrote:

In discussing these definite and vital figures I have often spoken as if we could be certain that Chaucer had in each case a definite individual in mind whose portrait he painted with scrupulous accuracy in every detail. I am, however, very far from feeling sure that this was true. It may very well be that in these vivid and lifelike portraits are mingled not only traits from more than a single individual, but even an indeterminate amount of purely imaginative construction. (74)

This is more cautious, and probably much nearer the truth. But, if imaginative touches and traits from more than one person were mingled in a characterization, would this characterization have been recognized as pointing to a definite individual? I think we must agree with Lowes that Manly has provided an illuminating commentary, but not proved his point.[23]

There are, of course, many instances in fiction of the portraiture of contemporaries. The Victorian novel-

[23] *Geoffrey Chaucer* (1934), pp. 200 ff. The quotation from Manly is by the kind permission of Messrs. Henry Holt and Co.

ists were free with it. But either personal relationship or satirical intent was usually the moving cause. The reflection in Thackeray's novels of his unhappy family affairs and his devotion to Mrs. Brookfield, or of his quarrels with other writers; the picture of Dickens's father as Mr. Micawber or of Leigh Hunt as Harold Skimpole—these belong in another category, aside from their ampler frame, from the vignettes of the Canterbury pilgrims. Though Chaucer is hail fellow well met with his company, he preserves a marked detachment. He looks at them objectively. This is an important point. The same appears to be true of most writers of fiction; when they are not living over private reminiscences or giving vent to personal rancor, they are under little temptation to make their creations close portraits, and are free to set them down as composites. J. P. Marquand, who certainly knows a good deal about his art, puts it thus:

Of course any writer in any field whatever, every time he sets down a sentence, is translating his observation of life as he has known it. But when it comes to drawing a character from life and setting his personality upon the printed page, nearly every writer whom I have ever met will tell you that no actual human being is convincing in this highly artificial environment. Living men and women are too limited, too far from being typical, too greatly lacking in any universal appeal, to serve in a properly planned piece of fiction. A successful character in a novel is a conglomerate, a combination of dozens of traits, drawn from experience with hundreds of individuals, many of them half known and half forgotten; and all these traits have been transformed by passing through the writer's mind. From a writer's standpoint it takes a vast number of disconnected memories and impressions to create a satisfactory illusion of reality.

Almost exactly the same idea occupies the preface of Bruce Marshall's *Father Malachy's Miracle.* Even an avowedly typical figure is not best presented photographically. Henry James wrote a notable short story, "The Real Thing," which demonstrates that in painting a close likeness of a social type is not as effective as an artificially constructed picture.[24]

The difference between Chaucer's method and that of the modern novel or short story is far less when the narrative of the journey to Canterbury is taken into account. As for the formal portraits in the *General Prologue,* it is clear that many elements have gone to their composition—many more than the casual reader suspects. They are subtly varied; sometimes externals are emphasized, as with the Yeoman; sometimes character, as with the Parson; sometimes both, as with the Prioress. Detailed descriptions get tiresome after a time (think of having twenty-nine of them!); Chaucer wisely kept many characters in the background, whence they could be drawn if need arose, and concentrated attention on some of the more picturesque ones. The Host's remarks often introduce personal description in the most natural way possible. Hitherto we have considered Chaucer's realism as derived from his own observation

---

[24] For the quotation from Marquand, cited with the kind permission of Messrs. Little, Brown and Co., see his *H. M. Pulham, Esq.,* Boston, 1941, pp. vii f. *Father Malachy's Miracle* was published in New York in 1931 by Doubleday and Co.

of life; it is also derived, to a degree astonishing to those
who have not considered the matter, from literary and
pseudo-scientific tradition, some of it of the most formal
sort. Character writing, with stress on moral qualities,
is as old as Theophrastus, more than two centuries before the Christian era. Medieval romance writers were
fond of bald catalogues of physical traits, especially of
the beauties of the gentler sex. Allegory frequently employed great realism in personified abstractions. Read
the account of the pictures on the walls of the Garden
of Mirth in the *Roman de la Rose.* The following may
be Chaucer's own translation of the description of
Avarice. Though it has more than once been cited in
this connection, it is too striking an illustration to omit.

> Another ymage set saugh I
> Next Coveitise faste by,
> And she was clepid Avarice.
>
> .   .   .
>
> And she was clad ful porely
> Al in an old torn courtepy
> As she were al with doggis torn;
> And bothe bihynde and eke biforn
> Clouted was she beggarly.
> A mantyl heng hir faste by,
> Upon a perche, weik and small;
> A burnet cote heng therwithall
> Furred with no menyver,
> But with a furre rough of her,
> Of lambe-skynnes hevy and blake;
> It was ful old, I undirtake.
>
> .   .   .

This Avarice hild in hir hand
A purs that heng [doun] by a band
And that she hidde and bond so stronge,
Men must abyde wondir longe
Out of that purs er ther come ought.

(207–243)

Langland sometimes treated allegory realistically, as in the scene when Glutton was minded to go to confession, but decided to turn into the alehouse, where he found Cis the shoemaker, Tim the tinker, Sir Piers of Pridie, Hugh the needle seller, Clarice of Cock-Lane, and others. Not without influence on Chaucer were the "physiognomies," popular pseudo-scientific treatises linking mental characteristics to external appearance and movement and connecting the whole with astrology. Thus, the Wife of Bath had wide-set teeth, and bore the marks of certain planets on her body; Mars and Venus were in conjunction at her nativity and were potent in forming her disposition. In short, Chaucer took his own where he found it, in life and books. And his descriptions differ from most medieval summaries in that they are not static; as has already been noted, his pilgrims in the *Prologue* are already moving along the road to Canterbury.[25]

He manages in an amusing way to seem to be eager to observe the common custom of arranging persons according to their station, and at the same time to violate

[25] "If Lessing had known the Canterbury Tales, he might have quoted the General Prologue as a telling illustration of his thesis in Laokoön, that time is the poet's sphere and space the painter's. Chau-

such schematization, in order to suit his purposes. "Kindly excuse me," he says in the *General Prologue* (743 ff.), "if I have not ordered my people according to their rank" (in hir degree). "You know I am rather stupid" (my wit is short). This is enough to put us on our guard. As soon as a proper beginning has been made with the most distinguished man in the company, the Miller, so drunk that he would "abyde no man for his curteisie," breaks in; the Reeve insists on having his revenge for the story about a carpenter; and the Cook follows. Take a look at the general arrangement of the pilgrims in the *Prologue*. Certain rough groups emerge. Sometimes the underlying principle is plain enough; sometimes it is not.

1	Knight	15 – 19	Five burgesses
2	Squire	20	Cook
3	Yeoman		
		21	Shipman
4	Prioress	22	Doctor
5	Second Nun	23	Wife of Bath
6, 7, 8,	Three priests		
		24	Parson
9	Monk	25	Plowman
10	Friar		
		26	Miller
11	Merchant	27	Manciple
12	Clerk of Oxford	28	Reeve
13	Man of Law	29	Summoner
14	Franklin	30	Pardoner

cer, exceptionally gifted with a retentive optic memory, saw the group of banqueting pilgrims before his mind's eye when he sat down to compose his Prologue. But since he used the poet's medium,

This does not follow the favorite procedure of classifying mankind according to feudal principles and setting forth the distinctive marks of each class, as in the "estates of the world" literature. Gower, in his *Speculum Meditantis,* presented "a general review of the various estates of human society, from the Pope to the labourer." [26] Chaucer never forgot his fundamental aim: to present in his *Prologue* an effect of unstudied realism. The same is equally true of the selection and arrangement of the tales that follow. The experiment of pressing them into a formal classification has been tried by Professor Tupper in his brilliant and learned attempt to make the Seven Deadly Sins in part the basis of choice.[27]

---

he was forced to describe in succession what he remembered having taken in at a glance, and thus the guests at the banquet, portrayed one after the other, assumed the garb and equipment that went with this single-file arrangement." A. J. Barnouw, "Painting and Poetry," *Germanic Review,* VIII (1933), 2.

For the passage from the *Romaunt of the Rose* (ll. 207 ff.) see Robinson, p. 666. H. R. Patch, "Characters in Medieval Literature," MLN, XL (1925), 1–14, cited this passage and gave other illustrations. For the scene in Langland see the B-text, Passus V, 304–326; *Piers the Plowman,* ed. Skeat, I, 158–160. For the physiognomies, W. C. Curry, *Chaucer and the Mediaeval Sciences,* New York, 1926.

[26] Ruth Mohl, *The Three Estates in Mediaeval and Renaissance Literature,* New York, 1933, esp. pp. 102 ff. For the quotation in regard to Gower see G. C. Macaulay, *Selections from the Confessio Amantis,* Oxford, 1903, p. xiii.

[27] Frederick Tupper, "Chaucer and the Seven Deadly Sins," PMLA, XXIX (1914), 93–128. J. L. Lowes, in an article with the same title, PMLA, XXX (1915), 237–371, strongly dissented. A list of Tupper's other publications on this subject will be found on p. 237 of Lowes's article, to which should be added Tupper's rebuttal, "Chaucer's Sinners and Sins," JEGP, XV (1916), 1–51. "All the Sins," says Tupper,

His views have been sharply questioned. But if they are
not acceptable in the form in which they were put forth,
they have been of service as showing how vividly the
Sins were present in Chaucer's mind, as, indeed, in the
mind of any writer of the fourteenth century. Criticism
is always the better for fresh and original theories, whatever the final view in regard to their validity may be.

Chaucer's literary devices are greatly aided by his
gaiety and high spirits, greater in the *Tales* than in any
other work. There seems little doubt that the poet, in the
quiet days in the country when he could spend leisure
hours with his books and his pen, was in truth in as
happy a mood as Chaucer the pilgrim and his associates.

"are presented by precept and example," and this treatment is "ar-
chitectonic"; it is "not casual but organic." Since medieval writers
divided each sin into various "branches," these branches—or even
their antitypes—may stand, argued Tupper, in place of the capital
sin. Thus, while the Pardoner illustrates Avarice and Gluttony directly, the Manciple illustrates Wrath, through its branch Chiding,
and the Doctor Lechery, through its antitype Chastity. Lowes pointed
out how great were the variations, in actual medieval practice, in
subdividing the sins, and denied that a man of Chaucer's day could
have recognized to which of the deadly seven a given subordinate sin
should belong, or be so classified through its antitype. There is much
force in this criticism. Writers were certainly wont to make clear
the arrangement which they followed. Perhaps it may be added that
it seems odd that if Chaucer built up his collection in part on the
structure of the Sins he concealed it so effectively that even modern
scholars, with their prying eyes, have never perceived it. The chief
reason, however, why the theory does not carry conviction is that
such a schematic arrangement is contrary to the general effect of
accident and spontaneity which Chaucer obviously tried to produce.
But I think that Lowes, in the ardor of controversy, hardly did
Tupper's work full justice.

Apparently joyous work may, of course, be done in illness or misfortune, as the lives of Hood and Lamb re-
mind us, and it might be maintained that Chaucer's
merriment is only a carefully calculated effect. But while
so long a work must have been composed under a variety
of emotional conditions, most readers will agree with
Raleigh that "his joy is chronic and irrepressible." [28]
Renoir remarked of the painting of Velasquez that "it
radiates with the joy the artist had in doing it." This
radiation is one of the secrets of the imperishable charm
of the *Tales*. The pilgrimage to Canterbury is a comedy
in the modern sense; it has often been called a Human
Comedy, in that it is a shifting kaleidoscope of life, but
I am here emphasizing its humor. Balzac, who gave
currency to the term "comédie humaine," had little
humor. There are, indeed, serious moments on the Canterbury road, some stories of tragic cast, but these are
clearly secondary to the main design, and in place as
dramatic contrast. Tragedy, since it appeals to the deepest emotions, must be wary of artificialities; it must treat
its theme directly and sincerely. It will, of course, make
use of accepted conventions peculiar to its age—the
chorus in Greek drama, the blank verse of Elizabethan
days, the rolling alexandrines of the classic French
theater. These did not seem unnatural in their own time.
Comedy, on the other hand, constantly and shamelessly
revels in tricks. We know that they are tricks, and do
not mind them if they are amusing. Farce, which no-

[28] Walter Raleigh, *On Writing and Writers*, London, 1926, p.
113.

body takes as a picture of life, employs them in fullest measure. Even when it depicts everyday scenes, comedy admits of greater departure from realism than tragedy. Exaggeration, heightening of the incongruity which is the foundation of humor, is inevitable.

Chaucer's fun often defies analysis; we are likely to find ourselves dupes of the master humorist. It ranges all the way from the saltiest jests to the subtlest innuendo, but when it becomes whimsical and elusive we must be on our guard. We search in vain elsewhere in the Middle Ages for such foreshadowing of the art of Lamb or Barrie. Frequently we cannot be sure whether the poet is joking or not. Consider one small point as an illustration, which has, indeed, been much debated. We are told of the Prioress that

> Ful weel she soong the service dyvyne,
> Entuned in hir nose ful semely.

Is this a sly dig? It has generally been so regarded, but well-informed scholars have been telling us that "this mode of nasal intonation is traditional with the recitative portions of the church service." [29] But is this the whole story? The Prioress is a lady whose affectations are slyly revealed. Her name, "Madame Sweet-Briar," and her dainty ways, contrast oddly with her large build ("hardily, she was nat undergrowe"), and her wide forehead ("it was almoost a spanne brood, I trowe"). She speaks fluent and stylish French—but of the Middlesex variety. She is a lady of exaggerated sensibility: she

[29] Robinson, p. 755, following Manly, ed. of 1928, p. 504.

bursts into tears if she sees a mouse caught in a trap, or if one of her little dogs, which were probably a nuisance, got smacked or went to the dogs' heaven. Yet the portrait is on the whole sympathetic, and there are no wicked asides when she tells her tale later on. Perhaps Chaucer originally intended to have a little gentle fun with her, and changed his mind when he decided to give her the pathetic tale of the murdered schoolboy, which contrasts vividly with the Shipman's jolly yarn preceding and the wild parody of the debased metrical romances which follows. But this is speculation. Cartoonists tell us that the most effective satire does not result from gross exaggeration, but from just enough distortion of some peculiarity to throw a face or a figure off balance. Sometimes it is hard to tell where portraiture ends and perversity begins. So it may be with the Prioress's singing. But if I were betting, I would put my money on the joke.

We must be wary of treating Chaucer's work in too mechanical a fashion; of assuming that its progress can be determined by the application of formal tests; that we can spy out all its secrets by taking thought and scrutinizing the text with a gimlet eye. Much must remain obscure. Chaucer is the last of poets to be captured easily by relentless logic. There has been a great deal of discussion as to what tales were already on hand, and utilized as the narrative of the journey progressed. Some direct evidence of satisfactory character does exist; the *Knight's Tale* and the *Second Nun's Tale* are clearly early work revised. Less direct evidence is often hazardous. Conventional treatment, for example, does not necessarily point to early composition. In the tales of the Man of Law and Monk such treatment is perfectly suited to the subject matter and forms an artistic contrast to the realism of other stories. In the *Melibeus* and the *Parson's Tale,* which seem very archaic, there are some reasons for assuming translation by Chaucer in the Canterbury period. French or Italian influence, another frequently invoked test for early dating, may well have affected the poet in his latest years. He certainly did not forget all that he had learned from foreign models. The composition of the pilgrimage probably covered only some twelve or thirteen years.

Caution must also be observed in trying to follow out changes in Chaucer's assignment of the tales. It is generally agreed that the Man of Law was not originally given the story of Constance; it is likely enough that he originally told the *Melibeus,* though there is no absolute proof of this. The *Shipman's Tale* was obviously first written for a woman, and best fits the Wife of Bath. But when we try to penetrate farther into Chaucer's earlier plans, we find little agreement among scholars. It is wisest for our purposes here not to attempt to penetrate. After all, his final decision was to give Constance to the Man of Law and the story of a deceitful wife to the Shipman. In considering the artistic effect which he intended, it is safest to follow his final arrangements. So it is with the order in which he filled in his design— a closely related subject. Our best knowledge must be guesswork, and should be treated as such. Theories, if often enough repeated, have a way of assuming the color of facts.

More will be said of these matters in Chapter IV. In general, I assume in this book that Chaucer first composed the *General Prologue* and then proceeded in order with the narrative of the journey, though, of course, with some utilization of older material, some shifting of assignments, and some skipping about. Such would be any poet's normal method of composition. Some difficult questions will present themselves, but one thing seems plain: any attempt to follow his earlier plans in detail will lead us into a bog of unproved conjectures. After all, we have to work with what he has left us.

◄§III. THE FABLIAU TALES

WE MUST NOW turn our attention to the tales which, to borrow an expression from Gamaliel Bradford, are "utterly guiltless of the odious flavor of necessary morals"—those of the Miller, the Reeve, the Friar, the Summoner, the Shipman, the Merchant, and the Cook. First of all, in order to have a clear understanding of the type to which these belong, it is desirable to review some well-known facts.

Literary classifications are, as we all know, unsatisfactory. Neither poetry nor prose fits well into pigeon-holes. This is particularly true of the larger forms, such as epic, lyric, and romance; the smaller ones, such as ballad, folktale, and lai, are more easily summed up. The fabliau, which is usually short, is remarkably distinct and definite. To be sure, it shades off into other types, borrowing here and lending there; it has obvious affiliations with the ballad, the apologue, the farce, and the coarse merry tale in prose. But its general and fundamental character is clear: it is an amusing tale in verse—"des contes à rire en vers"—as Bédier, the chief authority, has defined it.[1] A peculiarly French creation, it is gay and impudent, and indecorum is an almost constant characteristic; but mere obscenity, which is usually dull anywhere, is not very common. Of the seven fabliau tales in the Canterbury collection, only one, that

---

[1] Joseph Bédier, *Les Fabliaux,* Paris, 1925, p. 30 (and earlier editions). To this classic of scholarship every later worker is deeply indebted.

of the Friar, is entirely unobjectionable. While the *Cook's Tale* is only a fragment, the last line gives a strong hint of what is to come. The French form was regularly in octosyllabic couplets; it flourished in France from the middle of the twelfth to the first quarter of the fourteenth century. About a hundred and fifty specimens have survived; a great many others must have perished.[2] New ones occasionally turn up. It was particularly the expression of the middle class. Hard-headed, solid citizens were less and less inclined, as their own importance in the social order increased, to swallow aristocratic conventions and class distinctions or to accept rascality and stupidity in high places. Such targets the fabliaux attacked with a rollicking gaiety far more deadly than invective. Their mood was not so much satirical as irreverent. Satire usually implies moral fervor and desire for reform. The fabliaux show none of this; they attacked social pretenses, extortion, the frailty of women, the stupidity of cuckolds, the lustfulness of churchmen, mainly because such subjects were good for a hearty laugh.

Although designed rather for the tavern or the crossroads than for the castle hall, they sometimes came up in the world and were forgiven their vulgarity if it was amusing and kept in its place. Anything truly comic usually breaks down the barriers of caste. That fabliaux occasionally appear in courtly attire, giving themselves

[2] The standard collection is still that by Montaiglon et Raynaud, *Recueil général et complet des fabliaux des XIIIe et XIVe siècles*, 6 vols., Paris, 1872, etc.

aristocratic airs and graces, must not mislead us. In narrative art they had the advantage over the romances. Chivalric adventure in the longer forms, whether prose or verse, was almost always rambling and uncertain, straying down by-paths, fetching long digressions, losing the thread of the story in episodes. The lais were better managed, probably because they were short, but they were far less dramatic than the fabliaux. The ruder authors were particularly clever in presenting ingenious situations with a "snap" at the end, after the fashion of an O. Henry story, in subordinating details, and in suggesting movement through rapid and natural dialogue. On the other hand, character is seldom presented with any subtlety, and descriptions are usually brief and conventional.[3]

It is very important to observe that, according to all indications, the fabliaux never became popular in England or were much imitated in English. Coarse popular tales certainly existed before Chaucer's time, as attacks by the clergy and echoes in the ballads show, but few have survived. The closest extant example is *Dame Siriz,* a lively little version of the popular Oriental theme known to folklorists as "the Weeping Bitch." It shows strong English quality; while not Sunday-school stuff, it is not gross, and its tail-rhyme stanzas are not in the French tradition. The *Pennyworth of Wit* tells how a husband learns the virtues of a faithful wife and resists

---

[3] See the admirable essay by W. M. Hart, "The Narrative Art of the Old French Fabliaux," in *Anniversary Papers by Colleagues and Pupils of George Lyman Kittredge,* Boston, 1913, pp. 209–216.

the seductions of a mistress—a complete reversal of the
fabliau spirit, and quite English in its didacticism. A
similar transformation may be studied in English lyrics
based on French models.[4] A third little piece, *The Fox
and the Wolf,* is clearly best regarded as an offshoot of
the beast-epic, but its waggish tone and neat little plot
show the kinship between our type and episodes in the
Reynard the Fox literature.[5]

Just why this kind of story did not flourish on English
soil need not be discussed here; the striking fact is that
it did not. Its great prominence in the *Canterbury Tales*
is therefore all the more surprising. Here for the first
time, apparently, it really had a chance in English, and
it was greatly bettered in the telling. Particularly to be
noted is Chaucer's substitution of the five-stress couplet
for the French octosyllabics, which gave his verse more
elbow-room and greater ease, variety, and euphony.
Since no direct source for any of the seven tales mentioned above is known, study of what Chaucer actually
contributed is to some extent conjectural, and a special
problem in each case. Certainly, however, his transformation was very great. In some instances, as the
Reeve's Tale, relationship to a definite fabliau is marked;
in others, as the *Merchant's Tale,* we have to do with
widespread popular tradition. He also applied the
fabliau technique in some degree to other stories in his

[4] H. E. Sandison, *The "Chanson d'Aventure" in Middle English,*
Bryn Mawr, Pa., 1913.

[5] For an excellent discussion see the preface to *Middle English
Humorous Tales in Verse,* ed. G. H. McKnight, Boston, 1913. The
three stories here mentioned are printed in this volume.

collection. The *Pardoner's Tale,* in which three rascals are tricked, has the fabliau ingenuity of plot, rapid movement, and lively dialogue. The *General Prologue* and the narrative of the pilgrimage, with its vivid contemporary figures and their quarrels, must also be mentioned. The exact number of the tales showing fabliau influence is of no great moment; the important thing is that here, for the first time in English verse, so far as we can tell, a deliberate effort was made to take full advantage of the opportunities offered by the French *contes à rire.*

These lively yarns may well have had a special attraction for Chaucer, because he was getting a little bored with classical and romantic narrative. "In their main structure and substance," says Professor Mackail, "even where they deal with romantic stories and episodes, the *Canterbury Tales* represent the reaction from romance. Chaucer brought poetry into the open air, just when the romantic atmosphere was beginning to be oppressive." [6] He did more than this; he ridiculed the absurdities of degenerate romances in *Sir Thopas,* and inserted sly digs into the *Knight's Tale* and the legends of Cupid's saints. As for classical story, the Doctor's and the Manciple's retellings do not seem done with enthusiasm; they are among the weakest of the collection. In sharp contrast is the enormous gusto of the fabliau tales. Consider the Friar's narrative about the summoner who haled

[6] J. W. Mackail, *The Springs of Helicon,* London, 1909, p. 58. See also Agnes K. Getty, "The Mediaeval-Modern Conflict in Chaucer's Poetry," PMLA, XLVII (1932), 385–402. Germaine Dempster, *Dramatic Irony in Chaucer,* Stanford, Cal., 1932, has some good comments on fabliaux.

offenders into the archidiaconal court, and finally got lugged off to hell himself. How Chaucer does enjoy it! —the instant congeniality of summoner and devil; their sworn brotherhood; their mutual confidences as to business methods; the summoner's curiosity about the domains of Satan; and the devil's sly hint that he will soon know enough about them to lecture in a theological chair. All this is riotous fun, and the cream of Chaucer's art.

Of course he did not have to learn realism from fabliaux; a rich and varied career, which had brought him into close contact with all sorts of people, had given him the best of lessons. And it had had another important effect; it had made him a cultivated man of the world. The delicacies and subtleties which experience as well as art had given him were beyond the reach of the jongleurs. His superiority is particularly evident in the two points where, as I have already said, the fabliaux are weak: description and characterization. There is nothing in them to match the portrait of the carpenter's wife in the *Miller's Tale* (A 3233 ff.), or of the "myrie chiid" Absalom (A 3312 ff.), or the character drawing of the friar in the *Summoner's Tale*.

Probably Chaucer first became interested in the fabliaux not long before he began the *Canterbury Tales,* since there is no evidence of influence or imitation of them in his earlier work. It is true that since this work followed courtly or learned models, it was unsuited to the fabliau technique. But, on the other hand, he may well have regarded the loose-lipped tales of the jongleurs with a bit of the same disdain which aristocratic poets commonly displayed; only later perceiving, with increasing maturity, how interesting such narratives really were and what opportunities they offered for artistic development. The inescapable and important fact, I repeat, is that they make their appearance suddenly, in considerable numbers, on the Canterbury pilgrimage, told with all the freshness and enthusiasm of a new literary discovery. This quality must be felt rather than proved, but I do not think that any reader will deny it. Cheerful stuff befits this joyous holiday. The Merchant alone strikes a gloomy note, proper to the "wepyng and waylyng, care and oother sorwe" of that unhappy husband, and to the mordant irony of his contribution to the symposium on marriage. Of course Chaucer took satisfaction in more sedate types—the pious tale of the Prioress, the virtue story of the Man of Law, the saint's legend of the Second Nun, and so forth. But I do not see how anyone can read the fabliau tales without feeling that there he was letting himself go, as it were, as he never had before. Here was a golden opportunity for something new in English storytelling, and he was not the man to miss it.

But there were difficulties ahead. Could Geoffrey Chaucer, the ambassador, the courtier, the sober man of business, the "Socrates full of philosophy," the aristocratic versifier, the celebrant of the Saints of Cupid, the analytic novelist of the *Troilus,* appear as a writer of coarse popular tales, be they never so brilliant? What would his high-born readers and patrons think? What would the moral Gower and the philosophical Strode say? If the parallel is not too far pressed, it would have been a little as if Tennyson had turned from writing the *Idylls of the King* to versifying the *Contes drolatiques.*

Nothing is clearer than that poets who wrote for aristocratic circles greatly dreaded the accusation of introducing "vulgarity" into their works. Chivalric adventure, not low life, was for the attention of the highly born; *cortoisie,* not *vilainie,* the proper thing. Conversely, courtly tales were not for the ears of the common herd. Raoul de Houdenc, at the end of the twelfth century or the beginning of the thirteenth, says in the opening lines of his romance *Méraugis de Portlesguez:*

> Il n'i a mot de vilainie,
> Ainz est contes de cortoisie
> Et de beaus moz et de plesanz.
> Nus, s'il n'est cortois et vaillanz,
> N'est dignes dou conte escouter
> Dont je vos vueil les moz conter.[7]

Jean Renart, in the *Lai de l'Ombre,* at the end of the thirteenth century, begins his work (lines 4–11) with similar sentiments. "He who jests is a base fellow (*vilains*)": Jean is resolved to show his refinement (*cortoisie*) in an agreeable work in which there is neither scoffing nor insult.[8] In the thirteenth century Henri d'Andeli, a learned and cultivated cleric attached to the

---

[7] Ed. M. Friedwagner, *Raoul von Houdenc; Sämtliche Werke,* Halle, 1897, Vol. I, *Méraugis,* 27 ff.

[8] J. Bédier, *Le Lai de l'Ombre* par Jean Renart, Paris, 1913. I am indebted in this chapter for verification of quotations from Old French to Professor C. H. Livingston of Bowdoin College, though he is not responsible for my text.

cathedral at Rouen, took for his charming *Lai d'Aristote* a very popular droll story [9] in a pseudo-classical setting. Henri had only to look up over the door of his own cathedral to see an episode from it represented in stone. Its neatness of plot, irreverence, and sparkling humor are irresistible. But Henri was obviously not quite comfortable about it. The plot is familiar. Alexander is advised by his tutor Aristotle to resist the seductions of his mistress. She has her revenge; she displays her lightly clad body below Aristotle's study window, and lures him down into the garden. Finally she persuades him to play horse for her, so that she can ride about on his back. And then comes the "snap" in the story: when Alexander discovers him thus, and twits him with his infatuation, the sage retorts that he himself has been proved right, for if a woman can thus enslave an old man, how much more easily can she ensnare one burning with youthful ardor! So much for the story. In his introductory lines Henri shows his fear of offending his noble readers.

Now I will come back to what I am going to relate, a romantic story which I have undertaken, the subject of which I thought highly of when I heard the tale, which is to be set forth and expressed in rhyme and related without vulgarity (*vilonie*) or abbreviation, for a work through which vulgarity runs should never be recited at court. As long as I live, I will not seek to relate vulgarity in my writings; I have not

[9] See *FF Communications*, No. 74, "The Types of the Folk-Tale; a Classification and Bibliography"; Antti Aarne's *Verzeichniss der Märchentypen*, translated and enlarged by Stith Thompson, Helsinki, 1928. The student of fabliaux should become familiar with this book.

undertaken it and will not do so; vulgar words I will not employ in my work or in any *dit* that I compose, for vulgarity spoils everything, and detracts from its flavor.[10]

Elsewhere Henri has given us, as Bédier remarked, "un renseignement curieux: écrivant un grave *dit* historique, il nous fait remarquer que—ce poème n'étant pas un fabliau—il l'écrit sur du parchemin, et non sur des tablettes de cire. . . . On n'estimait pas que ces amusettes valussent un feuillet de parchemin." [11]

It must especially be emphasized, as I have already suggested, that such avoidance of vulgarity was a matter, not of morals, but of manners. In our own times, frank descriptions or representations of the sexual functions have been frowned upon, as exercising a stimulating and unhealthy influence upon the imagination, though we have been getting bravely over this in recent years. In the Middle Ages physiological processes were taken very frankly. Sex had few reticences; it was not paraded, but was accepted with no blushes as a part of normal human life. The same was true of the excretory functions. Sexual and scatological decorations, some of them irresistibly funny, were common in churches and cathedrals and in the decoration of pious volumes.[12]

[10] *Œuvres de Henri d'Andeli*, ed. Héron, Rouen, 1880, *Lai d'Aristote*, 39 ff. Another version of the lai was published by A. Héron, Rouen, 1901 (cf. *Romania*, XXX, 631). The exact meaning of *vilonie* is difficult to render in English.

[11] *Les Fabliaux*, p. 38. The poem referred to is *Le Dit du chancelier Philippe*, 255–258.

[12] See L. Maeterlinck, *Le Genre satirique, fantastique, et licencieux dans la sculpture flamande et wallone*, Paris, 1910; G.-J. Witkowski, *L'Art profane à l'eglise*, 2 vols., Paris, 1908.

Sermons, didactic manuals, and books of edification contained stories which were, according to modern standards, rankly indecorous. There was little domestic privacy, even in the houses of the wealthy or the dwellings of the nobility. In the *Reeve's Tale,* the miller, his wife, his grown daughter and the two students all sleep in the same room. Very revealing, too, is the little scene at the end of the *Summoner's Tale.* The friar has had a dirty trick played on him by a sick peasant from whom he has tried to extort money. So he runs off to complain to "the lord of that village," who is sitting at meat with his family. The lady of the house listens calmly. The friar does not hesitate to describe a coarse bodily function in her presence, and she takes no offense. Her comment is illuminating: "What can you expect of a yokel?" Or, to put it in her own words, "a cherl hath doon a cherles dede." The "lordes squyer," carving the meat, enters into the spirit of the joke and, equally unabashed by the presence of the lady, proceeds to an ingenious, but unrefined, demonstration of how the stercoraceous gift to the friar might, as the donor bade, be equally divided among all the members of the covent.

It would be a mistake, however, to oversimplify the situation. The attitude of poets in the bookish and courtly tradition varied greatly according to the individual, the country, and the period. And the attitude of audiences differed too. Chivalry had put the highborn lady on a ridiculous pinnacle, as a superior and delicate being. The rank odor of the common herd was not for her nostrils; vulgar matters were beneath her notice. The romances, which were to a great extent intended for the ears of ladies, portray a system of love unmoral according to our standards, but they contain very little that is objectionable to us. There are some bedroom scenes and some frank details, but these are not frequent or salaciously handled. Moreover, social taboos are constantly changing, and so it was in the Middle Ages. The decay of knighthood as a governing social force and the rise of the middle class were particularly operative in regard to what was socially permissible. The old conventions were in theory kept long after they had ceased to have real validity, but poets did not mind showing that they were not deceived by them. To call a spade a spade might not be good form in aristocratic writing, but one could nevertheless show that he knew what a spade really was. Custom still decreed polite reserve, but did not discourage sly attempts to ridicule it. An example or two will make this clearer.

No medieval vernacular poem was more influential or more characteristic of its century than the *Roman de la Rose*. Jean de Meun was temperamentally the last man to complete the unfinished work of the youthful Guillaume de Lorris, which is graceful, decorative, and unreal as a tapestry. A cynical, middle-aged bourgeois, Jean delighted in fulminations against royalty and nobility, the clergy, and especially women. This was more than temperament; it was an expression of the new spirit of reaction against chivalry and feudalism. But Jean was obliged, as a continuator, ostensibly to model his work on the very conceptions which he attacked. As a result, he oscillated between extreme conventionality and extreme realism. In one passage (15159 ff.) [13] he employs the good old excuses of an elegant author for the use of strong language:

> Si vous pri, seigneur amoureus,
> Par les jeus d'Amours savoureus,
> Que, se vous i trouvez paroles
> Semblanz trop baudes ou trop foles—

and goes on at great length, urging that his matter requires plain speech, citing Sallust to support him, with a phrase imitated by Chaucer, "the wordes moote be cosyn to the dede." [14] Then addressing the ladies, he tells them that if they find coarse words in his work, contrary to what they are accustomed to hear, they must not blame him; it is all to teach a lesson. What he really thought about frankness of speech may be gathered from the long passage in which Reason, a female figure who hinders the Lover in his quest for the Rose, sets forth her views. The Lover, who may be taken as representing the conventional attitude, reproves Reason for having used a word unsuited to a "courteise pucele" (6928 ff.), and Reason proceeds to set him right. Things God has created ought to be called by their proper names. If ladies in France don't do this it is because they are not

[13] I cite from the edition of E. Langlois for the Société des anciens textes français, Paris, 5 vols., 1914, etc. See the excellent discussion of the poem in Petit de Julleville, *Histoire de la langue et de la littérature française,* Paris, 1896, II, 105 ff., by Langlois.

[14] Jean's "Li diz deit le fait resembler" (15190) is Sallust's "facta dictis exaequanda sunt."

used to doing so, for the right names of things would please them if they were accustomed to them, and they would commit no fault if they did so (7131 ff.). The interminable arguments of Reason may be studied at the reader's leisure. On account of the extraordinary popularity of the *Roman,* Jean's work tended, even long after his death, to break down set conventions.

Evidences of this appear in the *Decameron.* Perhaps it would be more accurate to say that we catch echoes, in a time when social arrangements had greatly changed. Boccaccio's work is dedicated to the ladies, and it contains, in the epilogue, apologies for freedom of speech. Unseemly things may be expressed in decorous terms; truth must be reported; poets ought to have as much license as painters, historians, or philosophers; in daily life we use words that are not nice; nothing in the world is harmful in itself. All this does not ring quite true; Boccaccio protests too much. In his day the convention of shielding the delicate female from the gross touch of vulgarity was preserved, but appears in point of fact to have been rather a joke. Manners were pretty free in the Italy of the budding Renaissance. There is, indeed, nothing indecorous in the behavior of the young people in the *Decameron* who flee the plague, and this is expressly emphasized at the end of the tenth day. And, as we have seen, their amusements are decoratively rather than realistically set forth. But there is more than a hint as to how impropriety in the telling of the tales was regarded. It is not only the young men who tell gross stories; though the girls occasionally pretend modest confusion, they are sometimes quite as guilty. When Elisa, for example, relates as a pleasant diversion how a nun caught with her lover escaped punishment by showing that she knew that the abbess was guilty with a priest, we can see how far we have moved from the situation set forth in the *Roman de la Rose* a century earlier. Just how far the lowering of private morals went is a question; certainly the court at which Boccaccio wooed the beautiful but sensuous Maria d'Aquino was corrupt enough. Whatever we think of the ladies of Boccaccio's day, however, it is clear that the *Decameron* was intended for a wider audience. Petrarch, a man of austere virtue, saw this plainly. When he received a copy from Boccaccio, in 1373, he replied:

It is a very big volume, written in prose and *for the multitude. . . .* If the humour is a little too free at times, this may be excused in view of the age at which you wrote, the style and language which you employ, and the frivolity of the subjects, and of the persons who are likely to read such tales. It is important to know for whom we are writing, and *a difference in the character of one's listeners justifies a difference in style.*[15]

It is obviously very difficult to define absolutely the attitude of Chaucer's audience toward vulgarity. This audience was not confined to the court, as we have seen, and conditions in England no doubt differed from those in France and Italy. But that certain taboos were bind-

[15] Robinson and Rolfe, *Petrarch,* New York and London, 1914, p. 191. Italics mine.

ing is plain from the care with which Chaucer protected himself against reproach. This he did by two formal apologies in the course of the narrative and by the *Retraction* at the end, which I think have been somewhat misunderstood, and also by representing himself as the reporter of a pilgrimage which he must in duty bound describe accurately.

The first of the apologies is from the *General Prologue;* the second from the *Miller's Prologue.*

> But first I pray yow, of youre curteisye,   725
> That ye n'arette it nat my vileynye,
> Thogh that I pleynly speke in this mateere,
> To telle yow hir wordes and hir cheere;
> Ne thogh I speke hir wordes proprely.
> For this ye knowen al so wel as I,   730
> Whoso shal telle a tale after a man,
> He moot reherce as ny as evere he kan
> Everich a word, if it be in his charge,
> Al speke he never so rudelich and large,
> Or ellis he moot telle his tale untrewe,   735
> Or feyne thyng, or fynde wordes newe.
> He may nat spare, althogh he were his brother;
> He moot as wel seye o word as another.
> Crist spak hymself ful brode in hooly writ,
> And wel ye woot no vileynye is it.   745
> Eek Plato seith, whoso that kan hym rede,
> The wordes moote be cosyn to the dede.
> Also I prey yow to foryeve it me,
> Al have I nat set folk in hir degree
> Heere in this tale, as that they sholde stonde.   740
> My wit is short, ye may wel understonde.

What sholde I moore seyn, but this Millere
He nolde his wordes for no man forbere,
But tolde his cherles tale in his manere.
M'athynketh that I shal reherce it heere.   3170
And therefore every gentil wight I preye,
For Goddes love, demeth nat that I seye
Of yvel entente, but for I moot reherce
Hir tales alle, be they bettre or werse,
Or elles falsen som of my mateere.   3175
And therefore, whoso list it nat yheere,
Turne over the leef and chese another tale;
For he shal fynde yowe, grete and smale,
Of storial thyng that toucheth gentilesse,
And eek moralitee and hoolynesse.   3180
Blameth nat me if that ye chese amys.
The Millere is a cherl, ye knowe wel this;
So was the Reve, and othere manye mo,
And harlotrie they tolden bothe two.
Avyseth yow, and put me out of blame;   3185
And eek men shal nat maken ernest of game.

All this has a familiar ring. Here is the court poet's appeal for pardon, addressed to persons of gentle breeding ("of youre curteisye"), begging that his plain speech will not be set down to lack of manners ("vileynye"); the reminder that the Miller was a "cherl," and told a "cherles tale"; and that he and the Reeve both gave what might be expected of common fellows ("harlotrye"). In Chaucer's day a "harlot" was of course merely a person of low birth, of either sex. The exact meaning of "curteisye" and "gentilesse" is difficult to sum up briefly; obviously "curteisye" implied ability to use euphemisms

like a gentleman, avoiding vulgar phrases. Thus, the
Merchant apologizes for his plain speech (E 2350–1):

> Ladyes, I prey yow that ye be nat wrooth;
> I kan nat glose, I am a rude man,

when he refers to the lovers in his tale as acting (E
2362–3)

> In swich manere it may nat been expressed,
> But if I wolde speke uncurteisly.

And the Manciple excuses himself for "a knavyssh
speche," particularly the use of the word "lemman"
(H 205 ff.). But never in Chaucer's formal apologies is
there any suggestion that the loose tales may give offense
as being immoral in the modern sense.[16]

Ostensibly, the poet further threw a sop to aristocratic
feelings in the *General Prologue* by pretending to fear
that he had not arranged his characters in due order of
their rank (743 ff.), pleading the shortness of his wit. As
we have seen in the preceding chapter, this disclaimer
need deceive nobody, and probably was intended merely
as a gesture. Plain speaking is justified by arguments bor-
rowed from Jean de Meun: in a true report things must
be related just as they occurred. Observe that this occurs
in both apologies; also that the line already quoted, "the
wordes moote be cosyn to the dede," which Chaucer
lifted from Jean, is ascribed to Plato; and note the reference to the Scriptures. That the very words of the
pilgrims have been set down is so patently absurd that

---

[16] J. J. Jusserand, *A Literary History of the English People*, New
York, 1895, I, 326, appears to have misunderstood matters.

it can hardly have been intended for belief. But all this is made to serve the ends of Chaucer's sly humor. When he says that it pains him to have to report just what the Miller said, he puts the cream on the jest—his heart bleeds, [17] but he *must* tell the tale as he heard it. Finally, he ends with a flash of sturdy English common sense: "Don't take jokes too seriously!"

But what of the disavowal, in the *Retraction,* of "the tales of Caunterbury, thilke that sownen into synne"? Does this agree with what has just been said?

I think that it does, absolutely. This disavowal is likely to be misunderstood unless medieval theological convictions in regard to sin are kept clearly in mind, and the whole is read with especial care. First of all, it will be well to have the relevant passage in the *Retraction* before our eyes.

After asking the forgiveness of readers if he has put anything into the "litel tretys" (the *Parson's Tale*) preceding that might displease them, Chaucer continues: [18]

For oure book seith, "Al that is writen is writen for oure doctrine," and that is myn entente. Wherefore I biseke yow mekely, for the mercy of God, that ye prey for me that Crist have mercy on me and foryeve me my giltes; and namely of my translacions and enditynges of worldly vanitees, the whiche I revoke in my retracciouns: as is the book of Troilus; the book also of Fame; the book of the .xix. Ladies; the book of the Duchesse; the book of Seynt Valentynes day of the

[17] Reading with Robinson "M'athynketh" or with Manly "Mathynketh." Skeat printed "me thinketh."

[18] I believe that the *Retraction* is the poet's own work; for a discussion, see below, pp. 155 ff.

Parlement of Briddes; the tales of Caunterbury, thilke that sownen into synne; the book of the Leoun; and many another book, if they were in my remembrance, and many a song and many a leccherous lay; that Crist for his grete mercy foryeve me the synne. But of the translacion of Boece de Consolacione, and othere bookes of legendes of seintes, and omelies, and moralitee, and devocioun, that thanke I oure Lord Jhesu Crist and his blisful Mooder, and alle the seintes of hevene.

In bitterly regretting that he has not devoted his talents to moral and didactic writing instead of worldly vanities and in disavowing the latter, Chaucer was expressing a thought common in medieval theological works. The duty of a man who has been given knowledge and learning is to use them in the service of God. This is the meaning of the reference to "oure book": "Omnis scriptura divinitus inspirata, utilis est ad docendum, ad arguendum, ad corripiendum, ad erudiendum in justitia" (II Tim. iii, 16). So Chaucer returns thanks to the heavenly powers that he has translated Boethius and other devotional matter.

In the second place, we have to reckon with ecclesiastical disapproval of works glorifying sexual love. The section of the *Parson's Tale* dealing with the deadly sin of Lechery illustrates this admirably. There the commonplaces of love-poetry—the sight of the beloved, the sound of the voice, the exchange of kisses, and so forth— are called fingers on the hand of the Devil. From the theological point of view the love-conventions which underlie so much of Chaucer's earlier poetry were rank wickedness. So not only the *Troilus* is disavowed in the *Retraction,* but works which seem to us as harmless as the *House of Fame* (where tidings of "Love's folk" are concerned), the *Legend of Good Women,* the *Book of the Duchess,* and the *Parliament of Birds.* The lost *Book of the Lion* was in all probability a reworking of Machaut's *Dit dou Lyon,* an innocuous and graceful love-allegory. By "many a song and many a leccherous lay" is meant, I believe, such pieces as *Merciles Beaute,* the *Complaint of Venus,* and the "balades, roundeles, virelayes" mentioned in the *Prologue* to the *Legend.* The word "lay" as applied to a poetical composition always means in Chaucer something to be sung,[19] though of course it might be read from the page. Chaucer's lyric verse is never lecherous in the modern sense, but some of it might have seemed so to an ascetic churchman in that it exalted sexual love. By the reference in the *Retraction* to those of the Canterbury stories that "sownen into synne" we must understand, I believe, not only those based on fabliaux, which often make a joke of fornication, but also those which celebrate romantic love and teach no moral lesson. If such a lesson could be drawn, the Church looked with an indulgent eye upon profane and even obscene stories. They were tolerated, and, indeed, are often found in collections of exempla for use in sermons, because they got ready attention from listeners. But mere glorification of sexual love for its own sake was another matter. From the narrowly pietistic point of

[19] Tatlock and Kennedy, *A Concordance to the Complete Works of Geoffrey Chaucer,* Washington, D.C., 1927, pp. 508–509.

view of the *Retraction,* such tales as those of the Knight and the Squire, the Wife of Bath, and the Franklin, might be held to "sownen into synne." The phrase affords no evidence that Chaucer was specifically disavowing the fabliau tales.

Some readers, I imagine, may dissent from these conclusions. They will remember that medieval religion was not prevailingly gloomy, that it entered very deeply into cheerful daily life. They will also remember that many churchmen were not hostile to romantic pieces and that the preservation of such pieces is in large measure due to men trained in the scriptoria. They will ask if Chaucer could really be throwing aside tales and lyrics of the sort which had long been well-accepted courtly amusements. But I think that they should observe that the *Retraction* is a special kind of document, expressing the contrition and repentance and the submission to discipline enjoined upon a sinner intent on salvation; that what seems to us its exaggerated sensibility and phraseology may be paralleled in other instances; and particularly that it cannot be judged by itself alone, but must be considered in connection with the prologue and tale of the Parson. A full discussion of these matters is given in the concluding chapter.

When we turn from the apologies and examine the way in which Chaucer introduced his loose stories, we can see with equal clearness that he was making every effort to protect himself from the reproach of vulgarity. He disarmed objections and complimented his readers by setting a long and thoroughly aristocratic piece at the very beginning and by giving the place of honor as first narrator to the Knight. As has already been emphasized, Chaucer does not seem to have been primarily interested in romance at this moment. He did not write a new tale for the Knight, but furbished up an old piece, not always in a spirit of reverence, and one not wholly suited to roadside narrative—notice the Latin motto at the beginning. Having guarded himself thus carefully, he came to what he had been itching to do, and wrote the tales of the Miller and the Reeve and started on the Cook—and he had the time of his life. But the difficulty was that the Host might be expected, after the Knight had done, to call upon some other member of the company well up in social rank. Chaucer solved this very neatly by having the drunken Miller insist upon being heard. Mutual dislike of Miller and Reeve is carefully "planted" in the *Miller's Prologue* (A 3144 ff.), so as to prepare for the Reeve's immediate revenge. Then the Cook, another boisterous rascal who will not be denied, insists on his turn, and again the Host gives way. But there ought not to be too much of the fabliau kind of story, so the Host restores decorum by calling on that solid citizen the Man of Law, who recounts at length the woes of Constance, a contrast in subject matter, treatment, and verseform to what has gone before.[20]

---

[20] I am quite aware that it has been conjectured that Chaucer did not originally put together his material in the order in which it now stands. Many years ago Furnivall suggested that the *General Prologue* and the links were written after most of the tales had been composed, and Skeat held a similar view as to the *Prologue*. Tatlock has presented strong arguments to the contrary. Miss Ham-

It will now be evident, I hope, as I have suggested in the introductory chapter, that when the *Canterbury Tales* were projected, Chaucer was particularly interested in the fabliaux and desirous of experimenting with them in English, and that he may have selected a

---

mond believed that "the writing and framing of Miller and Reeve; the writing of Cook, Summoner (?), Pardoner," and the insertion of a "subsidiary group" of characters into the *Prologue* followed "the assignment or writing" of most of the more serious tales. This was doubted by Manly, and is indeed very dubious. Carleton Brown argued that Chaucer originally began the collection with the *Melibeus,* as the tale of the Man of Law. With all respect to a distinguished scholar and an old friend, this seems to me in the highest degree unlikely. Certainly *Melibeus* held values for the Middle Ages and interested Chaucer in ways difficult for us to understand readily today, but I cannot think that the "mirthe and solas" promised in the *Prologue* were ever first exemplified by this long moralizing allegory.

It seems to me, as I have earlier pointed out, that we have to work from the arrangement that Chaucer has left us, as far as this can be determined, not from unprovable hypotheses in regard to earlier intentions about which there is no agreement. This was Kittredge's procedure in discussing the tales that deal with mastery in marriage: "It is Chaucer's final design . . . that we are considering, not the steps by which he arrived at it" (MP, IX [1912], 446, note). The A Group is of course singularly unvarying in the MSS. The conclusion that Chaucer wrote the *General Prologue,* started off with the old *Palamon and Arcite* as the *Knight's Tale,* then wrote the stories of the Miller and Reeve and began that of the Cook seems natural and convincing. This does not exclude, of course, some later alterations and revisions.

For the references to Furnivall and Skeat and Tatlock's discussion see his *Development and Chronology of Chaucer's Works,* Chaucer Society, Second Series, 37, London, 1907, pp. 142 ff.; for Miss Hammond's views, her *Manual,* p. 257, and *passim;* for Carleton Brown's reconstruction, *Studies in Philology,* XXXIV (1937), 8–35. I discuss the *Melibeus* below, pp. 130 ff.

pilgrimage as a framework and managed this framework as he did in order to make the ribald stories seem to arise naturally from the situation, thus to protect himself from the reproach of having introduced vulgar persons and vulgar narratives to persons of taste and breeding.

These points have been stressed as a corrective to the common practice of failing to give due consideration to the loose tales in estimating Chaucer's achievement, or of slurring them over, or of apologizing for them. But such emphasis must not, I repeat, be carried too far. It is clear that when he projected a collection of a hundred and twenty stories the poet was giving himself the greatest possible freedom to tell any tale that interested him. On a pilgrimage he could bring forward any narrator he chose, by a little deft manipulation, or even introduce a new one, as he did the Canon's Yeoman. He could also devote himself to any kind of tale that happened to interest him, or to any dramatic situation arising from the comments and quarrels of the travelers. As he proceeded with his work, he occupied himself less with the fabliaux, though he did not give them up altogether. How far this was due to a cooling of enthusiasm and how far to desire for artistic variety, it is impossible to say. He had had his fun with them, and had managed a difficult situation with great adroitness.

I have had the less hesitation in treating the fabliau tales at length because, as is now pretty generally recognized, they are technically among his most brilliant achievements. Here he reaches out for himself and anticipates modern methods and modern artistry in an extraordinary way. It is a thousand pities that their subject matter has often prevented due recognition of this. But to those who find fabliaux distasteful, the poet's own advice still holds good: "Turne over the leef and chese another tale."

⋐§IV. THE SEQUENCE OF THE TALES

ETAILED INVESTIGATION of Chaucer's intentions as to the order of the tales may be said to have begun in good earnest with the researches of Henry Bradshaw, Fellow of King's College, Cambridge, and (1867) Librarian of the University. Bradshaw seems to have been more interested in wrestling with knotty bibliographical and literary problems than in writing about them,[1] but his methods and results were given careful consideration by F. J. Furnivall, who undertook the arduous task of editing selected manuscripts for the Chaucer Society. It is pleasant for Americans to remember that Furnivall's work was in part due to the urging and assistance of Professor F. J. Child of Harvard and that generous acknowledgment was made by the British scholar.

Furnivall's methods and results were set forth in a "Temporary Preface," published separately, which still deserves careful reading, and is amusing for its vigor and unconventionality.[2] He called attention to the variations

---

[1] For references to the publication of Bradshaw's work and comments see E. P. Hammond, *Chaucer; a Bibliographical Manual,* New York, 1908, pp. 165, 166, 277, 520. Some of the discussions in Miss Hammond's book are, after forty years, in need of revision, but her work is still of great use to the student. For later bibliographical aids see the Appendix below.

[2] "A Temporary Preface to the Six-Text Edition of Chaucer's Canterbury Tales, Part I, attempting to show the true order of the Tales, and the days and stages of the Pilgrimage, etc., etc.," by F. J. Furnivall, Esq., M.A., Chaucer Society, London, 1868.

in the order of the tales in the manuscripts, the moving
about of the prologues, the close linking of some tales by
material in the text, the absence of this in other instances,
the contradictions in the tales of the Second Nun and
the Shipman as to the sex of the narrator, and the obvious incompleteness of the whole work.[3] He saw very
clearly, however, the importance of the fact that the
tales fall into certain well-marked groups, within each
of which the order is on the whole reasonably constant.
Decision as to the order of these groups is assisted by
allusions to time and place in the progress of the journey,
either in the tales themselves or in the connecting links,
and by cross-references and allusions from one tale or
link to another. The most important of the earlier editions, that by Thomas Tyrwhitt (1775–1778), was a very
fine performance, in view of the editorial methods
prevalent in his day. Tyrwhitt printed the tales in the
sequence in the magnificent Ellesmere Manuscript, now
one of the treasures of the Huntington Library in Cali-
fornia. In this the Wife of Bath, the Friar, and the Summoner come after the Man of Law, but Furnivall, following Bradshaw, moved up the group containing the
Shipman, the Prioress, Chaucer himself (*Sir Thopas*
and *Melibeus*), the Monk, and the Nun's Priest, so that
these would follow the Man of Law. The main reason
was that if the Ellesmere order is followed, the pilgrims,
who seem at one point not far from Sittingbourne, forty
miles from London on the road to Canterbury, are
much later on, after many tales have been told, just en-

[3] *Ibid.*, pp. 9–11.

tering Rochester, thirty miles from London.[4] This is very queer indeed. Furnivall accepted Bradshaw's re-arrangement unreservedly. His own words should be quoted. "A happy hit! And it sets us free to alter the arrangement of any or all of the MSS, to move up and down any *Groups* of Tales, whenever internal evidence, probability, or presumption, requires it." [5]

Familiar as Furnivall's results are, it may be well for convenience to set them down in tabular form. His marking of the groups by letters of the alphabet was generally followed; another which he proposed, by Roman numerals, was not. It is far better today to keep to his time-honored alphabetical notation, no matter what sequence one favors, and thus avoid ambiguity. The fewer group-designations we have, the better. The division of B into B^1 and B^2 was, of course, due to the uncertainty just noted as to what speaker and tale should follow the Man of Law. Furnivall tentatively set down the journey as occupying three and one-half days; the first ending with Group A at Dartford (15 miles), the second with Group B^2 at Rochester (30 miles), the third with Group E at Ospringe (46 miles), with a halt in be-

[4] At the end of the *Wife of Bath's Prologue* (D 845 ff.) the Summoner promises to tell "tales two or thre Of freres, er I come to Sidyngborne," and this is done in part in his prologue and tale (D 1665 ff.), after the Wife and the Friar have finished. Then the Clerk, the Merchant, the Squire, the Franklin, the Doctor, the Pardoner, the Shipman, the Prioress, and Chaucer with his two stories, follow, after which the Host calls on the Monk, saying, "Loo, Rouchestre stant heer faste by!" (B^2 3116)—Rochester, ten miles nearer London than Sittingbourne!

[5] Page 22.

tween for dinner at Sittingbourne (40 miles), and the last day with Group I, the Parson being the last narrator before the arrival in Canterbury (56 miles).[6]

Group A : General Prologue, Knight, Miller,
          Reeve, Cook (fragmentary)
Group B[1]: Man of Law
Group B[2]: Shipman, Prioress, "Sir Thopas,"
           "Melibeus," Monk, Nun's Priest
Group C : Physician, Pardoner
Group D : Wife of Bath, Friar, Summoner
Group E : Clerk, Merchant
Group F : Squire (unfinished), Franklin
Group G : Second Nun, Canon's Yeoman
Group H: Manciple
Group I : Parson, Retraction

This arrangement of the tales was quickly adopted by leading Chaucer scholars and editors, and remained virtually unchanged for some fifty years, displacing the Ellesmere order, which according to the Chaucer Society lettering would be AB[1]DEFCB[2]GHI. On some points there was not full agreement, for example as to the time scheme, which I have mentioned, not because I believe it to be correct, but as illustrating Furnivall's general method. "All the allusions of the Tales," he wrote, "are consistent with the scheme of a 3½ days' journey, except the one difficulty of the afternoon of the Parson's Prologue." [7] There is a possibility that one or both of the final tales, those of the Manciple and the Parson, do not belong to the outward journey, but to the return to

[6] Cf. Furnivall, pp. 42–43.   [7] Page 41.

London.[8] If this be the case—I think it very doubtful—reckoning of the number of days consumed by Chaucer's company in getting to Canterbury will of course be affected, if such a reckoning must be made. As has already been urged in an earlier chapter, definite results in setting up a time scheme are questionable. Again, the C Group contains no allusions or references which serve to place it, and has no link at the beginning or end. Furnivall, admitting that it might go "on any morning," arbitrarily gave it the position after the Nun's Priest "to make the Tales of the Third Day not less than those of the Second." [9] Not everyone assented. Skeat, for example, believed at one time that it ought to go after the Squire-Franklin Group (F), though in his great edition he followed Furnivall; and Shipley placed it after Group A.[10]

Some further questionable points in Furnivall's procedure will be noted presently. For the moment, the important thing is to get a clear idea of his general method and to realize its significance for Chaucer criticism. No doubt his great and deserved reputation as an authority on early texts had much to do with its wide acceptance. Who that has had the good fortune to know him can forget his enthusiasm, his alert figure, his

[8] This is discussed below, pp. 160 ff.

[9] Page 42.

[10] Skeat, *Oxford Chaucer*, III, 434; Shipley, MLN, X (1895), 260 ff.; XI, 290 ff. It will be remembered that I am indicating the trend of earlier opinion. The contribution of Bradshaw and Furnivall now seems to be in danger of being forgotten, even in England; see H. S. Bennett, *Chaucer and the Fifteenth Century*, Oxford, 1947, p. 69.

sparkling eyes and snowy beard, his wide range of interests, and his generous assistance to younger scholars? As
a result of his work and Bradshaw's, readers were for the
first time given the Canterbury collection in a sequence
without glaring contradictions. Although much was
lacking to the complete picture which Chaucer would
probably have given had he lived, the design seemed
better revealed than in any manuscript.

As time went on, however, and the twentieth century
came in, there was an increasing feeling that more attention should be paid to the manuscripts. Although no one
of them might preserve the order intended by Chaucer,
might not some further indications of this order, so far
as he had himself determined it, be discoverable? Such
indications would supplement the internal evidence of
the progress of the journey, or perhaps modify it. For
example, Samuel Moore, an excellent scholar, argued
for the sequence CB^2, "since it is almost invariable in
the MSS," and does no violence to the logic of the pilgrimage.[11] But Moore did not think the printing of the
tales in any manuscript sequence advisable. Again, it
was felt to be disturbing that the only manuscript
(*Selden Arch. B 14*) presenting the order of Bradshaw's
"happy hit," which Furnivall adopted, is a poor and un-
trustworthy one.[12] Ought so radical a shift to be accepted
with no good manuscript to support it? And are Furnivall's internal indications really as important as he

[11] PMLA, XXX (1915), 116–123.
[12] Manly and Rickert, *Text of the Canterbury Tales,* 1940, I, 496,
call it "merely a bad 15 C edition of no textual authority."

thought, particularly in view of the evidence that the poet sometimes changed his plan as he went along?

Furthermore, the desirability of a more accurate text than that in Skeat's great *Oxford Chaucer* (1894 ff.)— an edition the value of which must not be minimized— was leading Professor Manly, Miss Rickert, and other scholars at the University of Chicago to undertake a critical examination of all the extant manuscripts. With this the problem of the sequence of the tales was naturally connected. Some tentative conclusions and the general method of procedure were outlined by Manly in his edition of the tales in 1928.[13] This book was not planned for experts, but "for use in senior high school and elementary college work." Much is omitted, and the text is expurgated. It contains an admirable sketch of Chaucer's life and a great deal of fresh material in the notes, but would not require mention here if it had not, in printing the tales in the Ellesmere sequence, marked a departure from the regular practice of the best editors for some sixty years,[14] and lent to this departure the authority of the leading scholar of the Chicago group. Whether such a procedure was wise appears very doubtful. There is considerable question as to how much reliance should be placed, in constructing a critical text, upon scribal authority. Twelve years later Manly admitted that the only evidence as to the order of the tales

[13] John Matthews Manly, *Canterbury Tales by Geoffrey Chaucer,* New York, 1928.

[14] Except for John Koch, *Canterbury Tales,* Heidelberg, 1915. In the excellent Globe Edition (London, 1898), A. W. Pollard had followed the order of the Chaucer Society.

as intended by Chaucer is "such as is given by various allusions in the text." [15] Certainly there is good reason why an edition arranged for elementary students should not be arranged in a sequence which makes a jumble of the journey to Canterbury.

The edition of Chaucer's complete works in 1933 by Professor F. N. Robinson, of Harvard, was a notable achievement, involving a great deal of expert and arduous labor. [16] It is extremely useful to student and specialist alike for its excellent text, its extraordinary amount of bibliographical information, and its carefully considered criticisms. Robinson decided that since Furnivall's sequence lacks manuscript support in the crucial instance after the *Man of Law's Tale,* which has just been described, it should be abandoned in favor of the Ellesmere order. He pointed out that this had sometimes been advocated by others, and followed by Tyrwhitt, Koch, and Manly. He was undoubtedly mainly influenced by Manly; he seldom differs from him. He kept the Shipman as the next speaker after the Man of Law, but placed the Wife of Bath's *Prologue* immediately after the epilogue to the tale of Constance. He retained Manly's division of the Tales into "Fragments" tagged with Roman numerals, bracketing, like him, the alphabetical listing. This has not been generally followed, and should, I think, be abandoned. Manly himself did not use the Fragment numbering in his critical text. In

[15] See below, p. 115.
[16] F. N. Robinson, *The Complete Works of Geoffrey Chaucer,* New York, 1928. I refer to it here merely as "Robinson."

the B^2 section it involves renumbering of the lines. Furnivall, it will be remembered, also listed "Fragments" under Roman numerals, according to his own scheme.

In 1940 appeared the long-awaited critical edition of the *Tales* by Professor Manly and Miss Rickert.[17] This was, of course, designed for experts, and indeed is difficult for anyone else to comprehend fully. Too high a tribute can scarcely be paid to these two devoted scholars for their indefatigable labor in this stupendous undertaking, which undoubtedly shortened their lives. It is an achievement of which America may well be proud.

Thus, after some hundred and fifty years since the days of Tyrwhitt, the wheel had come full circle, and the Ellesmere sequence seemed partially, at least, to have reëstablished its authority. But, as we shall see, there were powerful dissenting voices; some of the most eminent scholars expressed their disbelief. The good medieval practice of citing "auctoritees" seems, however, less important at this point than an examination of the merits of each case. The issue is very clear-cut: shall the best manuscript evidence or the logic of the journey be followed? We may first look a little more in detail at Furnivall's arguments, and then at Manly's. It will be

[17] John M. Manly and Edith Rickert, *The Text of the Canterbury Tales,* 8 vols., Chicago, 1940. The Ellesmere order is followed. The admirable review by R. K. Root, *Studies in Philology,* XXXVIII (1941), 1–13, will be found of great assistance in working with the text; also Germaine Dempster's "Manly's Conception of the Early History of the *Canterbury Tales,*" PMLA, LXI (1946), 379–415.

remembered that the present endeavor is to put into relatively simple form a situation which is extremely complicated, and one which can really be fully understood only if the fact of this complication is kept constantly in mind.

It is odd that the Ellesmere advocates have offered so little criticism of the method which they sought to displace. "Manuscript authority" has generally seemed to them sufficient. Fortunately, however, Manly himself made a very clear and brief statement.

The order of the *Canterbury Tales* established by the Chaucer Society and since adopted by most editors is not that of any of the manuscripts. It was based upon the assumption that although Chaucer had not finished writing all the tales called for by his plan, he had at least definitely settled upon the details of the plan and had brought all the parts that he had written into harmony with it. A minute study of cross-references, allusions to the time of day and to places on the road, would therefore enable the student to recover from the jumbled order in the manuscripts the order finally intended by Chaucer.

But these assumptions are very far from being true. There is a good deal of evidence that Chaucer had not made final decisions upon several of the extant fragments of his plan. It is generally admitted that several passages in the text belong to earlier stages of his work and are out of harmony with his latest intentions. Certain lines near the beginning of the "Shipman's Tale" are witnesses to an earlier intention of assigning that tale to some woman, just as the Second Nun's allusion to herself as an unworthy son of Eve indicates that her tale had not been properly revised to suit its teller. The clear implication of the words of the Man of Law is that his tale was to be in prose.[18]

Reference is then made to the discrepancy in time between the prologues of the Manciple and the Parson.

I do not think that this is an accurate statement of the assumptions upon which Furnivall worked for the Chaucer Society. He surely did not believe that Chaucer had *"definitely* settled upon the *details* of the plan and had brought *all* the parts that he had written into harmony with it." For he wrote: "Tyrwhitt's conclusion . . . is irresistible that the *Tales* as a whole were 'left imperfect' (iv. 120, *Int. Disc.* § iii)" and that their " 'defects and inconsistencies . . . can only be accounted for on the supposition that the work was never finished by the Author' (iv. 121, *Int. Disc.* § iv)." [19] Furnivall had called attention, moreover, to the very discrepancies which Manly cited, and, as we have seen, confessed that he could not make the time of the *Parson's Prologue* agree satisfactorily with what precedes.

A more valid criticism of Furnivall is, I think, that he did not make sufficient allowance for the fact that the pilgrimage is not real, but imaginary; that it is not a factual report, but a work of art; that its details are often thrown off merely for the sake of creating an impression of realism; and that one cannot, especially in view of Chaucer's shifts and changes, fit these details into any

[18] *Canterbury Tales* (1928), p. 77. Quoted by permission of Henry Holt & Co.
[19] *Temporary Preface,* pp. 10, 11; cf. p. 38.

hard and fast scheme. These matters have been discussed in an earlier chapter.[20] We have seen that a great deal was left vague and that if this had not been done the absurdity of the whole business of storytelling for some thirty people riding along a muddy road would have been all too apparent. A reader does not yearn for accuracy, but for amusement. These considerations do not appear to have been sufficiently weighed by Furnivall, who even argued that the Pardoner must tell his tale in the morning because "a draught of ale he might have felt the need of, but the bite on a cake means before-breakfast," or that

one must allow the Cook some miles' ride, either to get drunk or fall asleep in. Granting that he'd been flea-bitten all night, or in bed with some quean, yet the stir of starting and the morning-air would be sure to have freshened him up and kept him awake for some miles . . . Are the 8½ miles from Ospringe to Harbledown too much to allow the man to have got thoroughly drunk in . . . ? I think not.[21]

Furnivall's attempt to fit the journey into three days and a half is probably too neat for the incomplete and unrevised work which Chaucer left behind. Perhaps he may be censured, too, for attaching too much weight to the poor Selden Manuscript. That this preserves what appears to be the right order at one point—Man of Law, Shipman, and so forth—is not of much consequence.

But in one respect Furnivall seems to have been abso-

---

[20] See above, pp. 40 ff.
[21] *Temporary Preface*, pp. 25, 26, 35.

lutely right: in insisting, following Bradshaw, that the localities mentioned as the pilgrimage progresses must be in the proper order. The road to Canterbury was extremely familiar to Londoners; they would have spotted a mistake immediately. It is very striking that although there is almost no description of what might be seen along the road, the advance of the pilgrims is very definitely marked by the mention of "the watering of St. Thomas" (about a mile and a half from the Tabard Inn), of Depford and Greenwich, Rochester, Sittingbourne, Boughton under Blean, and "Bobbe-up-and-doun" (in all probability Harbledown), and that *these are all in the right sequence* except that Rochester follows Sittingbourne. This, as Tupper put it, "is like placing the American Rochester after Syracuse on a journey from Buffalo to Albany." [22] Robinson, however, remarks that "there are so many small discrepancies in the work that the misplacing of Rochester and Sitting-bourne may be regarded as a slip of Chaucer's own which he left uncorrected." [23] But it seems less like a slip than a somersault. And there is one great difference between this and other discrepancies which neither Manly nor Robinson seems to have perceived. The passage in the *Shipman's Tale* which points to a female narrator; the Second Nun's remark that she is a son of Eve; the Man of Law's statement that he will speak in prose—these cannot be due to manuscript displacement. Nor can the contradiction in time between the prologues of the Manciple and the Parson be due to this; the order

[22] JEGP, XXXIX (1940), 526.   [23] Robinson, p. 1005

of Groups H and I is constant. If, then, we insist on keeping the Rochester-Sittingbourne mistake on the ground of manuscript authority, we ought to see just what this authority is worth.

The lively little epilogue of the *Man of Law's Tale* [24] is a good test. Which pilgrim is here introduced as the next speaker? The Host first calls on the Parson—"this Loller heer wil prechen us somwhat."

> "Nay, by my fader soule, that schal he nat!"
> Seyde the Shipman; "heer schal he nat preche;
> He schal no gospel glosen here ne teche.
> We leven alle in the grete God," quod he;
> "He wolde sowen som difficulte,
> Or springen cokkel in our clene corn.
> And therefore, Hoost, I warne thee biforn,
> My joly body schal a tale telle,
> And I schal clynken you so mery a belle,
> That I schal waken al this compaignie.
> But it schal not ben of philosophie,
> Ne phislyas, ne termes queinte of lawe.
> There is but litel Latyn in my mawe!

These lines are certainly admirably suited to the Shipman,[25] and nobody, I suppose, doubts that they were written by Chaucer. But when we turn to the manuscripts, what do we find? Only the bad Selden makes the Shipman the speaker and the teller of the next tale. The Ellesmere and many others omit the passage en-

[24] B 1163–1190; Robinson, p. 90.
[25] F. Tupper, "The Bearing of the Shipman's Prolog," JEGP, XXXIII (1934), 352–372.

tirely. Most of those that do contain it make the speaker the Squire, to whom it is ludicrously inappropriate. "My joly body" and "my mawe," indeed! Such terms do not suggest that elegant youth. And the Squire has a genuine prologue of his own (F 1–8), prefacing his courtly romance, which is not at all the sort of story hinted at here. Six manuscripts assign the speech to the Summoner, to whom it is quite as unsuited. A man who would speak only Latin when in his cups and was fond of bawling out "Questio quid iuris?" would hardly say that there was little Latin in him. Moreover, the Summoner has a certainly genuine prologue, linking his tale closely to that of the Friar. One way of getting around the difficulty is to conclude that Chaucer must have canceled or rejected the passage.[26] This is possible, but we surely ought to be very cautious about throwing out patently genuine material.

The whole matter is further complicated by the apparent substitution of the versified woes of Constance for a prose tale, usually thought the *Melibeus,* for the Man of Law, and also by the probability that the present *Shipman's Tale* was originally designed for the Wife of Bath. Scholars have valiantly sought to trace the stages of Chaucer's changes, but no agreement has been reached. I have already expressed my belief that no certainty is possible. But two conclusions do emerge, both of them instructive for us at this point. The first

[26] Manly and Rickert, *Text of the Canterbury Tales,* II, 491; Robinson, p. 800. I do not forget that some scholars have defended the Squire and some the Summoner.

is that if we follow "manuscript authority" we have a choice of riding off in one of two directions, neither of which seems right, or of omitting the passage altogether, on the dubious theory that Chaucer decided to abandon it. The second conclusion is that if we shut our eyes to "manuscript authority" we have in the admirable and certainly genuine *Man of Law's Epilogue* a good transition to the Shipman, which we have strong reason for accepting in order to get the sequence of localities right.

One trouble with attempts to explain matters as involved as these seems to be that critics have often assumed that somehow or other a correct and logical solution can be reached through the all-too-scanty evidence at our disposal. Thus Tatlock, a very cautious scholar, adds after an elaborate series of hypotheses: "The above explanation should not be penalized because complicated, for the true history of the *Canterbury Tales* was probably more complicated than any account of it which will ever be written." But I think it may, perhaps, be penalized, not because it is too complicated, but because the chances of discovering its complications seem so slight. Like Lord Dundreary, we have to recognize that there are some things no feller can ever find out. Tatlock's later summary of the situation seems a wise one.

Even if we should not grant (as I believe we should) that Chaucer meant this link for the Shipman, it seems hard to deny that this junction is a happy way out, which the poet himself might well have adopted. If an editor does not take it, he must follow the procedure of one or other of the three last and cautious editors, Robinson, Manly, and Koch; and the fact that each of them follows a different procedure is suggestive of the unsatisfactory character of all. . . . It is doubtless cautious to follow the order in the best MS; but it seems a despairing solution if that is neither authentic, nor consistent, nor satisfying.[27]

Skepticism as to the advisability of arranging the tales in the Ellesmere sequence or in one derived mainly from study of the extant manuscripts is justified by the peculiar conditions under which Chaucer's own lost copies, and those which may have been in the hands of his friends in London, were probably assembled and transcribed after his death, and also by the special character of the collection, a very long work, consisting of many

[27] J. S. P. Tatlock, "The *Canterbury Tales* in 1400," PMLA, L (1935), 100–139; see esp. pp. 118, 132. This is a study of great importance. On pp. 113 ff. he discusses the coarse epilogue to the *Nun's Priest's Tale,* which deserves a word here. It certainly seems to be genuine, except the last two lines, which look like scribal patchwork:

> And after that he [the Host], with ful merie chere,
> Seide unto another, as ye shuln heere.

It was not Chaucer's habit to make his transitions in this indefinite fashion, having no direct connection with anything following. That this whole epilogue was rejected or canceled by Chaucer (Manly and Rickert, *Text of the Canterbury Tales,* II, 39; Robinson, p. 862) does not appear convincing. It seems more likely that he never wrote the final transitional lines. No matter whether the order of the Chaucer Society or of the Ellesmere MS is followed, there should be after the Nun's Priest some definite indication of the next speaker.

It will be remembered that Furnivall put the Physician and the Pardoner (Group C) after the Nun's Priest, mainly in order to fill out his time scheme, since there are in C no internal indications of time or place to guide us. Next he put the Wife of Bath, the Friar, and the Summoner (Group D), but it may well be that the best arrangement is for the Wife to follow the Priest.

different elements, some of which were apparently never integrated into the whole by the poet himself. In the editing of any early text, great stress is rightly laid at the present day on reproducing as accurately as possible the form in which this has come down to us. Conjectural emendations and rearrangements, however ingenious, are better rejected if it is possible to get along without them. But a good editor must, at the same time, consider very carefully how far the text which he is following is trustworthy, and make due allowance for the conditions under which it was produced. If he is working with Shakespeare, for example, he will not give so much weight to a bad printed copy as to a good one; he will not perpetuate, except in a rigid facsimile, errors obviously due to the ineptitude or carelessness of printers; he will reject nonsense and admit corrections which have gained universal sanction, like Theobald's "sanctified and pious bawds" in *Hamlet* or " 'a babbled of green fields" in *Henry V*. He may decide that it is best to print in a form found in no one early text, as in the standard editions of *Hamlet*.

Now we have in the *Canterbury Tales* an unusually difficult problem. "It is hard," says Tatlock, "to think of any work ever written, important or unimportant, which was intended as a unit and in which there is anything like so chaotic a condition in the early authorities." None of the extant manuscripts is wholly satisfactory. None contains all of Chaucer's genuine work. Not a scrap of his handwriting has been preserved. Some omissions and inconsistencies are due to the probability that he never finally revised the whole or to his own negligence in matters of detail, but a far greater number to the blunders and inspirations of early copyists. No one can tell just where to draw the line. Those fellows were obviously doing their best to reduce what lay before them to order and to make such transitions as they could. They had, of course, none of our modern feeling for the inviolability of an author's text. They knew that they were working with an important collection, but they did not realize that it was one of the world's great classics. So the most austere of modern editors must discriminate, and not canonize their mistakes and ineptitudes.

This will be clearer if we review briefly the state in which Chaucer left his manuscripts at his death and what was done with them. Here we must depend to some extent upon conjecture, but the main outlines appear reasonably plain.

In all probability Chaucer first wrote on loose sheets of paper or vellum. Possibly he may have occasionally used tablets coated with a thin covering of wax. A fair copy was then made by a scribe, and perhaps copies were also made of other first drafts. This would give the poet opportunities for correction and revision. He may have followed various methods, and it is unlikely that he expended the meticulous care on the *Tales* that he did on *Troilus,* a poem far more rigid in form and admitting far less spontaneity and improvisation. While some portions appear to have been in the hands of his friends in London, it does not seem likely that he released the collection for general circulation during his lifetime. He was too much of an artist to let a work go out with so many holes in it. The fragmentary condition of the *House of Fame* and the *Legend of Good Women* is quite another story; these are complete as far as they go, and there are no omissions, no missing transitions, no problems of sequence, except such as are raised in the two prologues to the *Legend*.

It must once more be emphasized that Chaucer can have worked on the *Tales* only intermittently, even after he had retired to the country and relinquished his post at the Customs. His leisure was of short duration; he was too experienced and valuable a man to be allowed to give up public affairs and public service. This has a very direct bearing on the problem of how far he had a definite general plan for the pilgrimage. He can hardly have been building his house absolutely at random, thinking that one day he would make the architecture consistent. The drama of the roadside shows how keen was his interest in the relation of the different tales. That an arrangement, consistent in the main, can be made of what he has left is a strong indication that some such arrangement was in his mind. But the Member of Parliament, the Clerk of the King's Works, the Deputy Forester of the royal park in Somerset had a great deal to occupy his mind and distract his attention. He could not carry all the details of his pilgrimage in his head with the accuracy dear to scholars, even had he thought it worth while to do so. If new ideas occurred to him, they could readily be incorporated in so fluid a narrative, even if they meant changes in what had already been written. Some fine day he would revise it all.

It seems probable that he continued in this fashion up to the composition of the *Parson's Prologue*. The puzzling questions which this prologue raises must be faced later. In December, 1399, he leased a house within the precincts of Westminster Abbey, and there, on October 25th, 1400, if the inscription on his tomb in the Abbey may be trusted, he died.[28]

What happened next? That Chaucer had long been at work on a great collection of tales must have been well known, arousing keen desire to see it in its entirety. This desire was rapidly satisfied. That the whole was unfinished, fragmentary, and probably unarranged seems to have made little difference, especially as the poet had written a kind of ending before the last story ("Now lakketh us no tales mo than oon"); the scribes were put quickly to work. As to how the "editorial" business was carried out, we know very little—only what can be gathered from study of the manuscripts and of the literary habits of the time. Leaves of paper or vellum very quickly pile up, so there must have been quite a formidable mass when Chaucer finally laid down his pen. It seems probable, then, that the *Tales* reached the copyists tied up in bundles or sections. This would in part explain the "groups" or "fragments" with which modern

---

[28] The best studies to consult for a review of Chaucer's work with his manuscripts and the copying of them are Manly and Rickert's *Text of the Canterbury Tales* and Tatlock's *"Canterbury Tales* in 1400."

editors struggle. The outside leaves of medieval manuscripts often got badly damaged or lost; it is conceivable
that some of the transitional links may have gone in this
way. It is also conceivable that some of these links may
have been on loose sheets, which were shifted about or
misplaced when Chaucer altered, in some cases, the
assignment of a teller to a tale. That he himself left any
external indications of the order which he wished his
sections to follow seems doubtful; if he had done so,
there would not be such chaos in the copied manuscripts.
The scribes, as has been said, apparently worked to some
extent from the extracts in private collections, which
may have differed in important respects from Chaucer's
revised drafts. There seems to have been in many cases
strong desire to get the tales copied off in such a sequence
as would conceal as far as possible the gaps and broken
transitions. The making of books in those days was a
trade, carried on by professionals who were anxious to
please their patrons and make a good profit from their
labors, though, of course, private and amateur copyists
must not be forgotten. It is easy to fancy two or three
"editors" putting their heads together and striving to
produce as complete and attractive a collection as they
could, while others struggled with the problem in other
ways. Gaps in sequence were remedied by alterations,
omissions, or the composition of patchwork links. On
the whole, there seems to have been more endeavor to
make neat transitions than to keep in the right order the
large structural outlines, as revealed by allusions to time,
place, and other details. This is easy to understand. Poe,

in *The Purloined Letter,* reminded his readers that large type spread across a map is less readily perceived than small type. So the excellent scribe of the Ellesmere Manuscript allowed the Rochester-Sittingbourne error to stand, though he was usually careful about immediate transitions. Moreover, the intimate knowledge of many small details scattered through a very long text which modern scholars possess cannot have been at the command of fifteenth-century arrangers. Possibly manuscript sequence was influenced by desire to give prominence to tales which would especially please, or to those with good introductory material. It has been ingeniously suggested that the error in geography in the placing of Rochester and Sittingbourne may have been due to desire to put the groups without a genuine head-link—B², C, G—as far as possible toward the end.[29] Furthermore, individual tales seem often to have been copied for their own sake, sometimes with the sections in which they occur, and the dramatic interest of the journey unobserved or neglected. As time went on and the manuscripts were copied and recopied, a bewildering variety of arrangements and selections resulted. Although some classifications may be made and some developments traced, construction of an accurate genealogical tree of all the principal extant manuscripts is impossible. We may better speak of a grove of trees, whose roots are inextricably tangled. The main point to be remembered at the present moment, then, is this extraordinary complexity, and the fact that no clear unbroken relation to

[29] Tatlock, "The *Canterbury Tales* in 1400," PMLA, L (1935), 129.

the work of Chaucer himself can systematically be traced.

However, minute examination and accurate description of the manuscripts [30] greatly stimulated interest in the possibility of reconstructing Chaucer's changes of plan in the assignment and arrangement of the *Tales*. There are fashions in scholarship as well as in dress, and this particular one was for a time very much in vogue. Thus, in 1933 Carleton Brown wrote: "The information gained from a detailed study of the MSS of the *Canterbury Tales* throws light not merely on the operations of the scribes but also in some cases enables us to perceive successive stages in Chaucer's arrangement of the Tales." [31] No investigator carried on such study with more acuteness and learning than Professor Brown himself, but this is a far more difficult business than decision as to whether the Ellesmere order or that adopted by the Chaucer Society is the better one to follow. That choice lay mainly in determining the position of Group B^2 with reference to Groups D, E, and F; the position of Group C being also a problem, but of secondary importance. Group B^2 deserves very careful attention on account of its length and its dramatic significance in the Marriage Discussion; Group C, containing only

[30] For this see Sir William McCormick, *The Manuscripts of the Canterbury Tales,* Oxford, 1933, and Manly and Rickert, *Text of the Canterbury Tales* (note especially 1, 9 ff.). In graceful recognition of the work of the British scholar, the Chicago volumes were dedicated to his memory.

[31] "The Evolution of the Canterbury 'Marriage Group,'" PMLA, XLVIII (1933), 1041.

two tales and having no connection with this Discussion, much less. The best manuscript and internal evidence supports the usually accepted sequence of the rest of the groups. But the game of attempting to raise the curtain and discover just how Chaucer's plans for his great collection were made and how modified; just what he altered, added, rejected, and transferred—this proved very alluring, and a vast deal of laborious study has been devoted to it. How far the game may be played with safety is not a matter on which anyone can dogmatize, but I think it is fair to say that despite very confident (and usually conflicting) claims from various quarters, very few final conclusions as to Chaucer's shifts and modifications have been generally accepted.

In 1909 Tatlock made a statement to which many scholars will, I think, agree today.[32]

I am so far from begging the question of a single authentic arrangement that I do not believe Chaucer ever put the poem together at all. But I do not see how we can doubt that he would have studied out the matter carefully had he lived to finish the work; that the mention of times and seasons, of places along the road, and of tales already told, indicates that he bore the subject in mind more or less all along; and that if we can devise an arrangement without serious inconsistencies, we are justified in preferring it to a self-contradictory one, and in accepting it as coming near Chaucer's intention, even though the one be the arrangement of no manuscript, and the other that of many. To do otherwise, it seems to me, attributes to the poet a slovenliness, a carelessness, and even

[32] *The Harleian Manuscript 7334 and Revision of the Canterbury Tales,* Chaucer Society, London, 1909, for the issue of 1904, p. 26.

a lack of seriousness about his work quite beyond anything else we can attribute to him.

To this may be added an excerpt from his conclusions in 1935.[33]

Chaucer probably left the *Canterbury Tales* mostly in his own informal draft, and without external indication of the order of the "groups." The chances are that he knew where he intended almost all of these to be placed, if not quite all, though he might have changed had he proceeded farther, or had he revised; and he has left many clear if not conclusive internal indications. . . . The order of the "groups" in the MSS. has no authority whatever. The order adopted by Furnivall and Skeat is as near as any which can be devised to what Chaucer seems likeliest to have intended, and is the best practically.

The section on the Order of the Tales in the Manly-Rickert volumes [34] (1940) represents a decided modification of Manly's earlier views.

Some scholars have attempted to establish a few typical arrangements [in the manuscripts] as having been made by Chaucer and to derive one of these from another. Inasmuch as the evidence of the MSS seems to show clearly that Chaucer was not responsible for any of the extant arrangements, there is no reason to discuss the arguments of previous scholars as to his reasons for changes. [p. 475] . . . Have we then any evidence as to the order of tales intended by Chaucer? *Only such as is given by various allusions in the text.* [p. 490] . . . In interpreting the allusions . . . as they stand,

[33] *"Canterbury Tales* in 1400," p. 133.

[34] II, 475 ff. Italics mine. This discussion should, of course, be read in full. Quotations by permission of the Chicago University Press.

we must, it seems, conclude with Professor Tatlock in the main. In arranging the blocks of tales in accordance with time and place, it is clear that Block A, including as it does the General Prologue, must come first. B^1 . . . is generally regarded by scholars as coming next. *It is further quite certain that Block B^2, with its allusions to Rochester, should precede Block D, with its allusions to Sittingbourne.* [p. 491]

Manly then continues:

Block B^2 should not, however, be connected with Block B^1, for it is clear that [the Man of Law's] Endlink belongs to an early stage of the development of Chaucer's plan and that he finally did not intend to use it for introducing and connecting with [the *Man of Law's Tale*] any tale now extant. [p. 491] . . . In Block C there is no time or place allusion which enables us to determine its proper position. [p. 492] [But since it is] always placed before B^2 by the early scribes . . . there is no objection to accepting this position and placing it between Blocks B^1 and B^2. [p. 492]

I do not think that the evidence is sufficient to enable us to conclude that the poet finally did not intend to connect the (admittedly genuine) epilogue of the tale of the Man of Law with any tale now extant. We cannot look into his mind; we can only speculate. Tatlock says: "By all appearance the speaker intended [at the end of the Man of Law's epilogue] is the Shipman . . . the *Shipman's Tale* stands without a prolog. Here is a tale in search of a prolog, and a prolog just suited to it in search of a tale." [35] The conclusion seems obvious: B^2 ought to follow immediately after B^1. And if Chaucer was not responsible for any of the extant arrange-

[35] *"Canterbury Tales* in 1400," PMLA, L (1935), 132.

ments, what authority do these arrangements have for placing the Physician and the Pardoner (Group C) between B^1 and B^2? None, certainly, that is decisive. One scribe or editor may have misplaced these tales, and been followed by other copyists. But all this is secondary to the striking fact that Professor Manly and Miss Rickert finally reverted to the position of Furnivall and the Chaucer Society that the various allusions in the text must be the deciding factor in deciding the sequence of the tales and that the allusions to Rochester and Sittingbourne are guides that cannot be neglected. Had these conclusions been reached earlier and adhered to in practice, a great deal of editorial confusion might have been avoided.[36]

[36] In the Manly and Rickert text the Ellesmere order B^1D is adopted, with the epilogue (bracketed) to the *Man of Law's Tale* in the form introducing the Summoner. In his edition of 1928 Manly omitted the epilogue in his text, but printed it in his notes from the Lichfield MS, which introduces the Squire, though Manly noted (p. 573) that "the whole passage is . . . unsuited to the Squire." Robinson printed the epilogue with the Shipman as promising a tale, but placed immediately thereafter the Wife of Bath's prologue and tale. Any one of these solutions will certainly puzzle the layman.

In the Bryan and Dempster *Sources and Analogues* (p. viii) it is expressly stated that the order of the tales adopted by Manly and Robinson "is followed as a matter of convenience to the user and is not to be construed as implying any opinion upon the question of the order contemplated by Chaucer." In her analysis of the Manly-Rickert edition (PMLA, LXI [1946], 396, note 91) Mrs. Dempster says: "I should have preferred to retain the original plan for this work [i.e., the *Sources and Analogues*], and follow the Skeat order."

As might have been expected, Tatlock's statements were not welcomed by those believing that intensive study of the MSS might reveal Chaucer's intentions as to sequence. Thus, Carleton Brown protested vigorously, in a very elaborate review of the Manly-Rickert

In the light of the foregoing review, it seems clear that the best way to arrange the tales and links in a volume intended for those who wish to read the *Canterbury Tales* as literature, not as a rigidly scientific transcript from the manuscripts, is that adopted by Furnivall, Skeat, and many subsequent editors. That sequence is therefore made the basis of the ensuing chapter, and followed elsewhere in this book.

---

volumes (MLN, LV (1940), 606–621; see esp. pp. 616 ff.). An addendum to this review was published in MLN, LVI (1941), 163–175. Brown's earlier paper, "The Evolution of the Canterbury 'Marriage Group,'" PMLA, XLVIII (1933), 1041–1059, should also be noted. His last contribution to the discussion, "Author's Revision in the *Canterbury Tales*," PMLA, LVII (1942), 29–50, is full of interest for the expert. I cite him as perhaps the ablest representative of his point of view. Other references will be found in the classified bibliographies.

✒§V. THE DISCUSSION OF MARRIAGE

To speculate as to how Chaucer's genius would have found expression had he lived in the days of Shakespeare is a pleasant exercise for the imagination. His writing often displays so much dramatic quality that we feel that he might in another age have been illustrious as a playwright. The action of the *Troilus* has been arranged as fifty subtly varied scenes, with skillful use of dialogue and monologue.[1] Some of the Canterbury stories—those of the Wife of Bath, the Friar, or the Pardoner, for example—can easily be made into lively little plays. The speeches may often be recast in dramatic form with little alteration, the narrative explanations appearing as stage directions or as indications of speakers. Frequently an episode may be treated in a similar way. Try the experiment with the *Canon's Yeoman's Prologue,* in the conversation between the Host and the Yeoman (G 583 ff.). The tale which follows offers a contrast, on the other hand, in being almost wholly narrative. Of course any rewriting of Chaucer's work injures it. Really satisfying drama cannot be produced by tinkering. Moreover, the poet's delicate comments and descriptions would be lost, and I do not think that we would sacrifice these for a wilderness of stage directions. The impersonality of theatrical form

[1] T. R. Price, "Troilus and Criseyde; a Study in Chaucer's Method of Narrative Construction," PMLA, XI (1896), 307-322. A. W. Ward, in *Chaucer* (English Men of Letters Series), New York, 1880, pp. 117, 124, 186, had emphasized the poet's dramatic sense.

necessarily excludes the delightful intimacy with which the storyteller takes the reader into his confidence. But strong dramatic quality in the *Tales* is constantly evident.

This reaches its height in the narrative of the pilgrimage. Harry Bailly and the more prominent travelers seem almost as much actors in a play as Falstaff and his crew in the Boar's Head Tavern. Their sharply differentiated characters and occupations lead to discussions and quarrels as acrimonious as those which distressed Dame Quickly. Naturally the vulgar folk are the most contentious, and thus lend themselves most readily to drama. They have little self-restraint; they blurt out their feelings on small provocation. Sometimes much is made of this, as in the exchanges between the Summoner and the Friar, or the Miller and the Reeve; sometimes it is lightly sketched in, as in the mutual dislike of the Cook and the Manciple. The Host's gibes at warmed-over pies and at parsley which once buzzed about the shop would certainly have been avenged in the tale told by the Cook, which was to have been "of an hostileer," had it been finished. But there is also comedy of a far subtler sort, played by pilgrims who can use the rapier rather than the bludgeon, who can pink an adversary with the joy and sureness of a Cyrano—the Wife of Bath, the Nun's Priest, the Clerk of Oxford, and Chaucer the pilgrim himself—in the Discussion of Marriage, which introduces a theme of perennial interest to all mankind, rich and poor, gentle and simple, layman and celibate. Here

Chaucer's art reveals itself in its fullest richness and deserves the most careful study.[2]

The Discussion has been set forth in masterly fashion by Kittredge.[3] He was the first to give it elaborate analysis and to show clearly the carefully designed dramatic interplay between the pilgrims who engage in it. What he said in regard to the tales which he treated needs little modification. It appears, however, that he told only part of the story, though critics still disagree as to what the limits of this story should be. It seems worth while to review this question in some detail.

Kittredge thought that the Discussion begins with the Wife of Bath, whose prologue opens Group D; that it is continued, after the Friar-Summoner interlude, which is not concerned with it, by the Clerk of Oxford and the Merchant (Group E); and that it is ended, after the tale of the Squire, which must be regarded as another in-

[2] For references to dramatizations of the tales of the Wife of Bath, the Clerk, the Pardoner, and of the *General Prologue* see Miss Hammond's *Manual*, pp. 298, 308, 295; D. D. Griffith, *A Bibliography of Chaucer, 1908–1924*, Seattle, 1926, pp. 24, 25; W. E. Martin, Jr., *A Chaucer Bibliography, 1925–1933*, Durham, N.C., 1935, p. 23. Percy Mackaye has constructed a play with a plot and dialogue of his own; *The Canterbury Pilgrims; a Comedy*, London, 1917. Reworking a classic is hazardous business. I do not think that this venture can be called artistically saisfactory.

[3] "Chaucer's Discussion of Marriage," MP, IX (1912), 435–467; in less detailed form in *Chaucer and His Poetry*, Cambridge, Mass., 1915, pp. 146 ff. Criticisms and disagreement by Koch, *Englische Studien*, XLVI (1912), 112 ff., and H. B. Hinckley, PMLA, XXXII (1917), 292–305. Neither of these seems important. Other essays will be mentioned presently.

terlude, by the Franklin (Group F). But there seems
no escaping the fact that the Discussion really begins
as a consequence of Chaucer's own *Tale of Melibeus,*
in the *Monk's Prologue,* which follows that tale (Group
B²); that it is continued, after the Monk has finished,
by the Nun's Priest; whereupon it is resumed after
Group C (Physician and Pardoner), if we place it at
this point, by the Wife of Bath.[4] After this we may follow Kittredge.

First of all it is important to get a clear idea of just
what the theme of the Discussion really is. What tales
shall it include? Convictions on this point have differed
widely, ranging from those of Koch, who would add
the tales of the Miller, the Shipman, and the Manciple,
to those of Miss Schlauch, who would consider only the
stories in Groups D and E.[5] It seems plain, however,
that the Discussion does not concern wedded folk in
general, or even, as Koch put it, "the good or bad influence of a spouse on her husband," but a special question: shall husband or wife dominate? Which shall have

[4] I have traced this in detail in "The Marriage Group in the *Canterbury Tales,*" MP, XI (1913), 247–258.

[5] John Koch (see note 3, above); Margaret Schlauch, "The Marital
Dilemma in the 'Wife of Bath's Tale,'" PMLA, LXI (1946), 416–430.
Miss Schlauch, whose views are always deserving of attention, also
thinks that "we may detect an original order E²D E¹ which deprives
the Wife of Bath of the honor of precipitating the debate." (430)
She depends for her conclusions on manuscript evidence, the weak-
ness of which has been shown in the chapter preceding, and on her
conviction that the original order which she discerns is better and
neater, which seems to me a dubious line of reasoning. We cannot
be sure that a work put together at different times and with a strong

the deciding voice in family affairs? Such supremacy is expressed by the frequently repeated terms "mastery" and "sovereignty." Clearly it was on this basis that Kittredge made his analysis.[6] Our business, then, is not with tales or arguments involving matrimony unless they turn on this particular topic. Much critical confusion might have been avoided if this point had been kept in mind.

This is no arbitrary modern limitation of our field; it will be remembered that the question of conjugal supremacy was a very common theme of medieval debate. One cannot say that Chaucer was dependent on any one source. Sometimes the subject was imbedded in satires on women, in learned or bookish form. In the Wife of Bath's prologue he drew, directly or otherwise, from the *Roman de la Rose,* the *Miroir de mariage* of Deschamps, the *Epistola adversus Jovinianum* of St. Jerome, the *Liber aureolus de nuptiis* of Theophrastus, and the *Epistola Valerii de non ducenda uxore* of Walter Map. And the common folk were quite as much interested in this topic as were their betters.

The emblematic strife for conjugal supremacy symbolized by a man and a woman fighting over a pair of breeches . . . was very popular in the Middle Ages; we see it appearing in the fabliau of *Estormi,* as in that of *Sire Hains and Dame Anieuse* . . . of Hugues Piaucelles, as well as in the miséricordes and sculptures of Rouen, of St. Denis, of St. Seurin

---

flavor of improvisation, will always fulfil the strict demands of logic and consistency, as the critic conceives these demands.

[6] See especially his article above cited.

(Gironde), of Presles (Seine et Oise), of Auxerre, of Ville-franche, of Rouergue, etc., etc.[7]

Nor should the part played by sermons be forgotten. The ears of laymen were constantly assailed from the pulpit by reminders that a woman was the cause of the fall of Adam and that the wiles of women are responsible for many of man's later transgressions.[8] The transition from this to outright popular satire was easy. Failure to take account of these facts has led some critics to take misogynistic passages in Chaucer's work as reflections of his own personal experience.[9] There is no valid evidence that his marriage was unhappy.

I must also insist upon the importance of determining the proper sequence of the groups of tales in any consideration of the Discussion. Kittredge said: "We may profitably study the tales in groups, without regard to disputed problems of order," but on the very next page and thereafter he assumed a definite sequence: "the Marriage Group begins with the Wife of Bath's Prologue and ends with the Franklin's Tale: the order is Wife, Friar, Sumner, Clerk, Merchant, Squire, Franklin."[10] This is, of course, the traditional order, and few

[7] L. Maeterlinck, *Le Genre satirique, fantastique et licencieux dans la sculpture flamande et wallonne,* Paris, 1910, p. 206. Notice the illustration.

[8] See G. R. Owst, *Literature and Pulpit in Medieval England,* Cambridge, Eng., 1933.

[9] Masefield thinks that Chaucer's marriage was one "of the utmost and liveliest horror" (John Masefield, *Chaucer,* New York, 1931, p. 27).

[10] *Chaucer and His Poetry,* pp. 146–147. He took a similar position in his more extended argument in MP.

will quarrel with it. That the Wife of Bath is preceded
by the Nun's Priest (followed by the Physician and the
Pardoner, if Group C is placed here), not by the Man
of Law, is an equally essential point, which has been
discussed in the preceding chapter. It will be recalled
that Group C may very likely not have been intended
by Chaucer to follow Group B², if, indeed, he placed
it at all, that it contains no cross-references or indications
of time or place, and that Furnivall put it where he did
in order to fill up a short day. It appears highly probable
that the Wife of Bath should follow directly after the
Nun's Priest. The immediate linking of her prologue
with what precedes is lacking; the transitional lines
were apparently never written. But she deals with precisely the same theme as does the Nun's Priest, the sovereignty of woman, and in a similar spirit of controversy.
He had satirized it; she defends it. But Kittredge was
very positive that "the Wife of Bath's Prologue begins
. . . a new act in the drama. It is not connected with
anything that precedes. . . . It is the Wife of Bath who
starts the debate. . . . There is no connection between
the Wife's Prologue and the group of stories that precedes." [11] He was probably a good deal influenced by the
fact that the Physician and Pardoner preceded in the
texts current when he wrote; the urge to adopt the Ellesmere sequence had not then begun.[12]

[11] In his article above cited, 439, 467; in his book, 185.

[12] Before I published my article in *Modern Philology,* I sent it to
Professor Kittredge, and asked him if there was anything in it to
which he objected. With his habitual kindness, he urged me to print
it as it stood. In March, 1913, he wrote to me as follows. "What I

One thing is certain: the Discussion, whatever view we take of it, is no tight group, no frozen block. It is now and then interrupted by stories and conversation on other subjects. Just as Kittredge treated the Summoner and the Friar and the Squire, as providing interludes in the portion of the *Tales* which he considered, so we may regard the Monk, and, if we choose, the Physician and the Pardoner, as interludes in what comes earlier. The drama is heightened by allowing some of the pilgrims to nurse their outraged feelings until the proper time comes for a crushing reply. And Chaucer was too resourceful a musician to harp too constantly on one string. It is certainly hard to know where to place the Physician and the Pardoner. Perhaps the position between the Priest and the Wife is as good a solution as any, and it has the merit of long acceptance and incorporation in most texts. If, however, we decide to put it elsewhere, and not call it an interlude at this point,

---

meant, of course, was (as is the fact) that the Wife of Bath's Prologue is not joined to anything at the beginning—it starts a fresh group, with no back reference, no transition, no link. . . . I accept (tentatively) your contention that the Marriage Group is prepared for —that there is a Prologue to the Play, so to speak—though I don't think there is any *link* (actually written) between Prologue and Play."

Of course I agree that the link is missing. Whether we call the *Melibeus*, the *Monk's Prologue,* and the *Nun's Priest's Tale* (with its prologue) a Prologue to the Play or an integral part of that Play seems of no great consequence. The essential point, I think, is that the Wife's long harangue is not a bolt out of the blue, or the matrimonial discussion which follows, the airing of a new subject.

the connection between Priest and Wife will be much more obvious.[13]

All this will be clearer if we turn directly to the text. The Discussion may be arranged as follows, with the "interludes" bracketed.

$$B^2 \begin{cases} \text{Chaucer } (\textit{Melibeus}) \\ [\text{Monk}] \\ \text{Nun's Priest} \end{cases}$$

$$C \begin{cases} [\text{Physician}] \\ [\text{Pardoner}] \end{cases}$$

$$D \begin{cases} \text{Wife of Bath} \\ [\text{Friar}] \\ [\text{Summoner}] \end{cases}$$

$$E \begin{cases} \text{Clerk} \\ \text{Merchant} \end{cases}$$

$$F \begin{cases} [\text{Squire}] \\ \text{Franklin} \end{cases}$$

It will be instructive to glance first at the stories of the Shipman and the Prioress and at Chaucer's tale of *Sir Thopas,* which precede the *Melibeus* in Group B^2.

The *Shipman's Tale* is a good illustration of a story involving marriage, but not concerned with the Discussion now before us. It is fabliau stuff, on the common theme of the deceived husband, but its ingenious little plot, of a type familiar to students of traditional story,

[13] It is interesting to note that Lowes believed that "the Wife of Bath's Prologue and Tale immediately follow the *Nun's Priest's Tale*." PMLA, XXX (1915), 365.

has nothing to do with the question of marital supremacy. The merchant has no suspicion of the trick that has
been played on him, and is only disturbed lest the monk
has taken offense. Nor is there any suggestion of the
debate on "maistrye" in the Host's comments which
follow, with their warning not to trust monks.

It is easy to guess why Harry Bailly next calls on the
Prioress. He is naturally anxious to give precedence to
the gentlefolk, but he has hitherto succeeded in bringing forward only the Knight and the Man of Law; the
ruder fellows have demanded the right to speak, and had
their way. The Prioress is a lady of consequence, and
perhaps, with gentle dignity, has held somewhat aloof,
especially during the coarser tales, but she "gladly" as-
sents to the summons. Her pathetic little story, which
forms a sharp and no doubt designed contrast to what
has gone before has, of course, nothing to do with matrimony.

In order to restore the gaiety of the pilgrimage, the
Host now turns to Chaucer, rallying him on his constant [14] abstraction, his ample waistline, and his with-
drawal from the badinage of the company. "What sort
of fellow are you, always looking on the ground, as if
you would spy out a rabbit? . . . Tell us a tale of

[14] Dr. T. A. Knott has maintained ("A Bit of Chaucer Mythology,"
MP, VIII [1910], 135–139) that the poet's manner and his "elvish"
look are temporary, the effect of the touching story told by the Prioress. But "evere" cannot mean "at this moment," and there are other
reasons for disbelief, which I have already set forth (PMLA, L [1935],
90, note 25). Like many a humorist, Chaucer is a reflective observer
and falls easily into abstraction. The passage is discussed in detail
by R. M. Lumiansky, *Philological Quarterly,* XXVI (1947), 313–320.

mirth!" And Chaucer readily complies. However, the "deyntee thyng" which he tells has dangers in it for the autocrat of the wayside, who has been appointed "juge and reportour" of the tales; he has been called the first English literary critic whose utterances have reached us. But his ignorance makes him vulnerable. Partly in retaliation for his gibes, Chaucer, the accomplished man of letters, first presents him with *Sir Thopas,* a wild parody of some of the current English metrical romances—not of the type as a whole, but of those which ran into absurdities.[15] He is about as able to appreciate such delicate satire as a bull is to admire a

[15] The arguments of Miss Winstanley and of Professor Manly to prove, respectively, that *Sir Thopas* was meant to be a satire on the Flemish patriot Philip van Artevelde, or on the Flemings in general, do not appear convincing (Lilian Winstanley, *The Prioress's Tale and the Tale of Sir Thopas,* Cambridge, Eng., 1922, pp. lxv ff.; J. M. Manly, "Sir Thopas, a Satire," in *Essays and Studies by Members of the English Association,* Oxford, 1928, xiii, pp. 52–73). Manly thought that satire of the Flemings was Chaucer's "primary object." I have criticized this in detail already ("Satire in *Sir Thopas,*" PMLA, L [1935], 81–91). There are no direct allusions to Philip or the Flemings. Sir Thopas is said to have been born "at Poperyng," but Philip was not born there. "Popering" is a silly-sounding name to English ears, as Mercutio's raillery reminds us; it may have been chosen as a "birthplace" on that account. *Sir Thopas* cannot have been inserted in the *Tales* before 1387 at the earliest, and probably was much later. Philip died in 1382; the visit of the Flemish embassy to London, which Manly believed a prime cause for Chaucer's ridicule, took place in 1383. It does not seem probable that the poet would have satirized a man long since dead or a political event long past. The absurd picture of Sir Topaz, the jewel of knighthood, is amply explained by a reading of some of the degenerate English verse romances. There are excellent comments on this whole matter by Mrs. Loomis in Bryan and Dempster's *Sources and Analogues,* pp. 486 ff.

flower, and pronounces *Sir Thopas* "rym dogerel," as indeed it is, bidding the poet to tell something "in geeste," or to stop rhyming and offer something pleasant and profitable in prose. "Gladly," says Chaucer,—"I will tell a little thing that ought to satisfy you. If it doesn't, you are certainly hard to please!"

It is hard for us nowadays to understand why Chaucer thought the *Melibeus,* a long and—as it seems to us—dull affair, worth translating.[16] Certainly he was not, for the sins of the Host, punishing the reader by inflicting on him absurdity or boredom, as some critics have thought. First of all we must remember the very great popularity of didactic allegory in the Middle Ages. Chaucer, despite his modernity, was a man of his own day, and his work in general shows how highly he valued maxims and citations and the wisdom of earlier generations. But there is a very special reason why this particular piece would have been timely. It is in effect an exposure of the horrors of war and a plea for agreement among enemies. Albertanus of Brescia, the author of the Latin original, had fully experienced such horrors; he was also a judge and a citizen much concerned with public affairs in thirteenth-century Italy. His allegory is a strong plea for ending strife through conciliation and legal arrangements. In the reign of Richard II this would have been of especial interest. There is little

---

[16] What follows is more fully discussed in an article of mine, "The Tale of Melibeus," *Essays and Studies in Honor of Carleton Brown,* New York, 1940, pp. 100–110. See also Gardiner Stillwell, "The Political Meaning of Chaucer's *Tale of Melibee," Speculum,* XIX (1944), 433–444.

direct comment on current political events in Chaucer's work, but he must, like Gower and Langland, have felt keenly the evil results of prolonged international strife.

But there is more to be said than this. Although almost smothered by long speeches and learned citations, the *Melibeus* tells a story, which is important, for from it is derived the theme of the Marriage Discussion, and from it stems the Debate which follows.

A young man named Melibeus had a wife Prudence and a daughter Sophie. In his absence three enemies entered his house, and attacked his wife and daughter. Upon his return his wife advised him to have patience, and to ask the advice of his friends and relatives as to what course to take. This he did. Many advised vengeance, but the wiser ones counselled caution. Dame Prudence urged him not to be over-hasty. He answered that he would not be guided by her, especially on account of the danger of following women's counsels; "certes, *if I governed me by thy conseil, it sholde seme that I hadde yeve to thee over me the maistrye;* and God forbede that it so weere!" Thereupon Dame Prudence defended her sex and the excellence of the advice of women, at great length, citing many authorities to support her. Finally Melibeus gave in; ". . . wyf, by cause of thy sweete wordes, and eek for I have assayed and preved thy grete sapience and thy grete trouthe, *I wol governe me by thy conseil in alle thyng.*" Later he twice assured her of his complete subjection to her authority. She then gave him much further good advice, and sent for his enemies and persuaded them to promise him such satisfaction as he wished. He finally forgave them completely, thanking God "that hym sente a wyf of so greet discrecioun." [17]

The point of this greatly abbreviated analysis is clear. Give your wife the "maistrye," and all will be well. It is only a part of the story, and not the most important part, but it is just the issue which Chaucer chooses for a dramatic turn after the tale is done. The Host has a termagant wife, and the better fortune of Melibeus hits him in a sore spot.

> I hadde levere than a barel ale
> That goode lief, my wyf, hadde herd this tale! [18]
> For she nys no thyng of swich pacience
> As was this Melibeus wyf Prudence.
> By Goddes bones! whan I bete my knaves,
> She bryngeth me forth the grete clobbed staves,
> And crieth, "Slee the dogges everichoon,
> And brek hem, bothe bak and every boon!"

Harry Bailly is a man of simple wit, who first of all takes the *Melibeus* not as an allegory or a thing to be valued for improving maxims, but as a story. It is not strange that what stands out in his mind after Chaucer has finished is the patience of Dame Prudence, so great a contrast to the rampings of his own Amazon spouse, who has not been mentioned earlier, but whose tantrums may certainly be supposed to be known to the guests of the Tabard Inn. Thus Chaucer the pilgrim has scored again

[17] Quotations (Robinson), pp. 204, 206, 224. Italics mine.
[18] Robinson reads "Goodelief" as a proper name. But see above, p. 47, note 20.

off the Host for gibes about his absent-mindedness and corpulence, and Chaucer the poet has made the *Melibeus,* almost too heavy for roadside entertainment, the beginning of the liveliest discussion of the whole journey. A flick of the hand, and the conjuror has brought quite a different rabbit out of the hat.

In thus picking out a feature of the story which Albertanus did not much emphasize, and which he himself, in all probability, did not think important when he made the translation, Chaucer was, of course, following good medieval practice. A tale was good for any point that could be squeezed out of it. One of the hardest things for the modern reader to comprehend is the passion of the Middle Ages for taking simple matters metaphorically, for deriving from them secondary and often apparently dubious significations. Students of the *Divine Comedy* must be alert for four meanings: the literal, the moral, the allegorical, and the anagogical. The Scriptures were a magnificent riddle; the universe a complicated manifestation of the Divine purpose. So it was even in the simple stories told from the pulpit; one is often astonished at the far-fetched and complicated "morals" which were hauled by the horns out of the *exempla.* There is nothing far-fetched, however, about making female domination a central theme in the *Melibeus;* it is there, as plain as a pikestaff.

Finally, after his frank exposure of his bitter experience with marriage, the Host turns to the Monk, and—perhaps to relieve his feelings—indulges in some pretty tasteless joking about celibacy. "Every tonsured man should have a wife! You religious folk can make better payments to Venus than poor shrimps like us!" But the Monk, though he must obey the call to tell a tale, or suffer the heavy forfeit, does not retaliate. His "tragedies," though they deal occasionally with husband and wife, as those of Sampson and Midas, do not emphasize the question of conjugal supremacy or of the excellence of woman in counsel.

The case is quite otherwise with the Nun's Priest, whose graceful and amusing tale of Chanticleer and Pertelote brings forth some of the most acid of all the comments on the woman question. He is barely mentioned in the *General Prologue,* and there is little description of him in the link preceding his tale.[19] It looks as if Chaucer had brought him forward at this point in order to provide a counterblast to the exaltation of woman in the *Melibeus.* The Priest is under the thumb of a woman who is far above him in social and ecclesiastical rank. He is treated with little consideration; he jogs along on an ill-favored nag, while the lady's little dogs get fine bread and the best of attention. The Host rubs it in; there is no reason why he should be tender of the feelings of this fellow, who appears to be of little consequence. But he does not know his man. The Priest is very human and very adroit and very dangerous. He has contained his feelings through the

[19] For the inconsistency between the three priests in attendance on the Prioress in the *General Prologue* and the one here, see above, p. 45.

Melibeus, the Host's unsavory jests about churchmen, and the long procession of tragedies told by the Monk, but now his golden hour has come. The whole point of his story is that a husband who follows the advice of his wife will come to grief—just the reverse of the moral of the *Melibeus.*

> My tale is of a cok, as ye may heere,
> That tok his conseil of his wyf, with sorwe,[20]
> To walken in the yerd upon that morwe.

But this is not all. The Hen is ridiculed; her poor little scrap of learning from Dionysius Cato is completely buried under the Cock's copious citations. At one point, indeed, the Priest lets his feelings run away with him, and bursts out:

> Wommennes conseils been ful ofte colde;
> Wommannes conseil broghte us first to wo,
> And made Adam fro Paradys to go,
> Ther as he was ful myrie and wel at ese.

Then, recollecting himself, and perhaps feeling the disapproving eye of his lady mistress fixed on him, he hastens to add:

> But for I noot to whom it myght displese,
> If I conseil of wommen wolde blame,
> Passe over, for I seyde it in my game.

He ends his tale in good pious fashion, as if it were to be taken as an exemplum on the evils of trusting flatterers. But he did not need to emphasize his point fur-

[20] An abusive epithet—"curse her!"

ther. His bolt at the sovereignty of women had been shot.[21]

It is especially significant that Chaucer appears to have deliberately altered the story to fit the Marriage Discussion. The best modern opinion is that his source was either the Old French *Roman de Renart* or a version close to it. In that poem the Hen warns the Cock of danger from the Fox, but he disregards her counsel. In Chaucer's tale the Hen pooh-poohs her husband's fears, and the Cock, though warned by dreams, the significance of which he upholds as pointing to future events, finally takes his wife's advice and for this reason nearly comes to grief.[22]

When the Wife of Bath begins, Professor Kittredge must be the commentator. His clear-sighted and enter-

[21] I have here summarized, with some changes and additions, a part of my article in *Modern Philology*. The view that the symposium on marriage begins before the Wife of Bath has her say was reached independently by Professor J. S. Kenyon before my own analysis, but not printed. In "Further Notes on the Marriage Group in the *Canterbury Tales*," JEGP, XV (1916), 282–288, he pointed out that in the Nun's Priest's narrative Chaucer expanded greatly by the introduction of "auctoritees," put in the "Mulier est hominis confusio" joke, virtually changed a story of a Cock and a Fox to one of a Cock and a Hen, and reversed "the conventional rôle of scepticism towards dreams, making Chanticleer and Pertelote exchange places in this respect." He also believed that the Wife should follow directly after the Priest.

[22] This was, I think, first emphasized by Professor Kenyon (see preceding note). It is elaborated by J. Burke Severs, "Chaucer's Originality in the *Nun's Priest's Tale*," *Studies in Philology*, XLIII (1946), 22–41. He believes that the tale should be linked to those in the later Marriage Group on the one hand, and to the *Melibeus* on the other—just what I had contended for thirty years earlier.

taining pages should be read in full. I will add a few
comments of my own, but his analysis must be kept
clearly in mind.

A great deal of the opening portion of the Wife's
prologue is taken up with a defense of intercourse as
against virginity. But this is not the thought with which
she begins.

> Experience, though noon auctoritee
> Were in this world, is right ynogh for me
> *To speke of wo that is in mariage.*

How then is marital happiness to be attained? The final
point of the Wife's long harangue is that this will come
by letting woman have the mastery—precisely the conviction to which Dame Prudence converted Melibeus.
And this is also the point of her illustrative tale. The
Wife knows all about this. Her methods were not subtle;
notice how much they were like those of the Hostess of
the Tabard Inn, set forth in the *Monk's Prologue* earlier
(B^2 3080 ff.). She made things hot for her five husbands ("myself have been the whippe"). And she is
unblushing about it.

> For, God it woot, I chidde hem spitously.
> Now herkneth hou I baar me proprely,
> Ye wise wyves, that kan understonde.
> Thus shulde ye speke and bere hem wrong on honde;
> For half so boldely kan ther no man
> Sweren and lyen, as a womman kan.

It was a deliberate program. Women ought to learn the
art of taming men, as she did her husbands.

> I broghte it so aboute by my wit
> That they moste yeve it up—

The culminating episode in the prologue shows how she got the better of husband number five, the clerk Jankyn. He was fond of sitting by the fire at night and chuckling over a book containing stories about wicked women, as is the fashion of clerks.

> For trusteth wel, it is an impossible
> That any clerk wol speke good of wyves,
> But if it be of hooly seintes lyves,
> Ne of noon oother womman never the mo.

But this is not, I think, a "rude personal assault" on the Clerk of Oxford, as Kittredge suggested. Why should the Wife, even in badinage, insult that modest student, who has given her no provocation? It is a hit at the Nun's Priest, who has bitterly satirized women, and their claim to rule the affairs of the household. "Clerk," of course, means not only "scholar," but primarily "cleric, one admitted to a religious order; ecclesiastic." [23] Well, the time came when the Wife could stand Jankyn's reading no longer; she ripped a leaf out of his cursed book, they came to blows, and (after a rich description which must not be spoiled by a paraphrase) she finally put him in his place.

> But atte laste, with muchel care and wo,
> We fille acorded by us selven two.
> He yaf me al the bridel in myn hond,
> To han the governance of hous and lond,

[23] Robinson, Glossary, p. 1063.

And of his tonge, and of his hond also;
And made hym brenne his book anon right tho.
And whan that I hadde geten unto me
By maistrye, al the soveraynetee,
And that he seyde, "Myn owene trewe wyf,
Do as thee lust the terme of al thy lyf;
Keep thyn honour, and keep eek myn estaat"—
After that day we hadden never debaat.

Precisely the same issue closes the Wife's tale. The Loathly Lady finally gains dominion over her husband.

"Thanne have I gete of yow maistrie," quod she,
"Syn I may chese and governe as me lest?"
"Ye, certes, wyf," quod he, "I holde it best."

And so the result of this, says the Wife, was that they lived happily ever after.

The Discussion is interrupted at this point by the quarrel between the Friar and the Summoner, and their illustrative stories, but is resumed by the Clerk, the Merchant, and the Franklin.

The Clerk and the Squire are, with the exception of the Knight and the Franklin, the most attractive of all the pilgrims who have been given full-length portraits. Perhaps some of us would include the Prioress among those exceptions, but it is noticeable that the Clerk and the Squire suffer none of the sly thrusts which gently satirize that excellent lady. They are the "yonge, fresshe folkes" for whom Chaucer had obvious affection; the Squire, as he "guessed," was twenty years old, and the Oxford student may be thought of as near that age. They represent, respectively, two of the greatest interests of the poet's life: the Clerk, his devotion to books and study and "moral vertu"; the Squire, his absorption in poetry and romance. As a young man he had himself, as a page at court and as a soldier on the Continent, seen a good deal of the glittering externals of chivalry and had become familiar with the precepts of *fine amor*. Since the Squire does not touch on the question of "maistrye," his tale may be considered an interlude in the Discussion, but it is nevertheless more closely related to the surrounding tales than a casual reading may reveal. It will be best, however, to consider this later, and return to the Clerk.

The row between the Friar and the Summoner has given no pilgrim a chance to reply to the Wife of Bath's masterful defense of women, her savage onslaughts on men, and her side-thrusts at clerks. But now, by one of those happy inspirations with which Chaucer occasionally endowed Harry Bailly, the Oxford scholar is summoned to tell a tale. At first he gives little indication that he is going to defend his sex and those in orders and theological study; the Nun's Priest may even be disappointed at his seeming moderation. But his retort to the Wife is a deadly one. From his story of the patient Griselda, submissive to her husband in all things despite her sufferings, he first draws the unimpeachable moral that mankind should be patient under the afflictions sent by God. Then he suddenly addresses the Wife,

> Whos lyf and al hire secte God mayntene
> In heigh maistrie, and elles were it scathe—

and ironically exposes the results of following her precepts. His envoy [24] is an apostrophe to "noble wyves, ful of heigh prudence." The upshot of it is: Don't be humble, but take the reins in your own hands; be strong as camels or savage as tigers; make your husband jealous, and he will couch like a quail—in short, "lat hym care, and wepe, and wrynge, and waille!" That is what married life is like when woman has the sovereignty.

An astounding confession from the Merchant follows. He is not the man to unbosom himself in public, but his "experience" has been so bitter that he breaks out into a savage attack on wedlock, reinforced by an equally savage tale of a silly old husband deceived by his young wife. The Merchant has been married only

[24] Kittredge's warning that the words "Lenvoy de Chaucer" are a mere scribal rubric, that the envoy is spoken by the Clerk, is important. He compares the mistaken "Auctor," E 995. See his article, p. 449, note 2.

The arguments of Helge Kökeritz ("The Wyf of Bathe and al hire secte," *Philol. Quarterly*, XXVI [1947], 147-151) to show that Kittredge's interpretation of the last stanza of the *Clerk's Tale*, preceding the Envoy, is mistaken and that the word *secte* there means "sex" do not seem to me supported by the evidence. Chaucer does not use *secte* with this meaning in any of the other four occurrences of the word in his works (Tatlock and Kennedy, *Concordance*, p. 778). He does use it once, just as Kittredge here took it, in the sense of "a body of adherents to a belief," in the *Squire's Tale*, 17-18:
   "As of the secte of which that he was born
   He kepte his lay [belief, creed], to which that he was sworn."
In Chaucer's translation of Boethius the word *sex*, not *secte*, is used to distinguish gender: "sexes (*that is to seyn, male and femele*)" (Book IV, Prosa 6, Robinson, p. 431). Italics and parentheses in the text. Kittredge interpreted the passage—as, of course, should be done— from the Clerk's point of view, which was that adherents to the beliefs of the Wife of Bath were heretical.

two months, and he has discovered that his spouse is shrewish, malicious, and cruel. If the Devil himself were married to her, she would get the better of him. The Clerk had given the view of a scholar, accustomed to relying on authorities; the Merchant, though he can cite them too—Theophrastus, Seneca, Cato, and the Bible—speaks from bitter personal knowledge. The Wife of Bath is thus refuted on both counts.[25]

The unfinished *Squire's Tale* is pure romance, of the rich Eastern variety. There is no place in it for the question of marital sovereignty and no hint of anything of the sort is the little outline at the end of Part II of events still to come. But the selection of the Squire as the speaker at this point was not accidental. The Clerk and the Merchant have voiced bitter misogyny; the Squire follows the code of courtly love, as is proper for an elegant youth. According to that code, woman was a wholly virtuous and faultless being, while the lover was a poor worm, whose chief hope must be to excite her pity for his wretched state. As the familiar lines in the *General Prologue* tell us, the Squire has born himself well in soldiering "in hope to stonden in his lady grace," and he loves so desperately that he sleeps no more at

---

[25] How little the earlier Chaucer scholars realized the dramatic interplay of these stories is illustrated by the comment of Richard Morris, who took the Merchant's bitter irony as an evidence of Chaucer's "high estimation of women" and his "perception of a sacred bond . . . in true marriage between man and woman" (*The Prologue, the Knight's Tale, the Nonne Preestes Tale*, Oxford, 1895, xviii).

night than a nightingale. He is a fashionable Romeo in pursuit of a Rosaline. That his tale represents the artificial and decorative concept of love appears to mean that at this point Chaucer was preserving the dramatic balance by weighting the scales in favor of the gentler sex.

There seems no doubt that, as Kittredge urged, the Discussion of Marriage is designedly resumed and closed in the *Franklin's Tale,* with the solution that mutual forbearance and not "maistrye" is the key to marital happiness. How else is the long and detailed emphasis upon this in the opening lines (F 745–802) to be explained? Such emphasis is not necessary to the story; a simple statement would have shown the strong love between Arveragus and Dorigen, even had this not been revealed by his letters and her great sorrow during his absence. Domination has no part in happy wedlock. Wise lovers will instead practice "gentilesse," the considerateness which comes of good feeling and good breeding. This is the pivot on which the story turns. Arveragus and Aurelius and the Clerk of Orleans all displayed it; which of the three, the poet asks was the most generous? Again and again "gentilesse" is emphasized (F 1524, 1527, 1543, 1595, 1608, 1611).

Thus, the Marriage Discussion is brought to an end, and Chaucer takes up other matters, in the tales of the Second Nun, the Canon's Yeoman, the Manciple, and the Parson.[26] We have, of course, only a small part of

[26] That the *Parson's Tale* touches upon marital quarrels does not contradict this. That tale is, of course, a translation of homiletic ma-

his completed design, but even had he carried it farther, it seems doubtful if he would have returned to this particular debate. Happily, this part of the *Tales* is finished.

---

terial, and in such material exhortations to husbands and wives to live in amity were common. The Issue in the *Manciple's Tale* is not "maistrye" but "jangling"—failure to bridle the tongue (H 309 ff.).

◄§ VI. THE ENDING OF THE TALES

According to the familiar lines in the *General Prologue* (790 ff.) each pilgrim—and this must include Chaucer himself—was to tell two tales on the way to the shrine of St. Thomas and two on the return. But this ambitious plan was only about one-fifth completed. It seems fair to assume that there would also have been some account of the stay in Canterbury and of the night at the Tabard Inn after the pilgrimage was over, when the great question as to which tale was the best of all would have been decided and a supper given in honor of the fortunate narrator. The whole work, had it been finished, would have been much longer than the *Decameron*. There would have been about a quarter again as many tales. In many cases Chaucer greatly elaborated and expanded his connecting material, while Boccaccio's transitional passages are brief, excepting those at the end of each decade, when a day of storytelling is over.

The *Tales* are, however, definitely finished—after a fashion. It is clear that whatever may be the sequence of the earlier stories, the Parson is the last to have his say. All the evidence, both of manuscripts and of subject matter, points in that direction. It is also perfectly clear from the *Parson's Prologue* that the tale following (not really a tale at all) was intended to be the last of all when that prologue was written. We shall look at this in detail in a moment. Why, then, did Chaucer

give up his original scheme, and make this sudden end?
To this question may be added others already suggested
in the introductory chapter. Are the stories of the Manciple and the Parson to be understood as told on the journey to Canterbury or on the return to London? How
are the curious discrepancies in the time of day when
these two narratives are told to be explained? How can
the indications of place be reconciled with the amount
of storytelling on the last day? Is the *Retraction* genuine?
If so, does it reflect literary convention or personal conviction?

In order to make the discussion clearer, I will give
immediately my own conclusions. These are matters
about which we cannot dogmatize, but we have to make
up our minds as best we may in the light of the evidence.

I believe that Chaucer worked intermittently on the
Canterbury collection without making any radical
change in his general scheme until after the *Manciple's
Prologue* was written, and, presumably, the present
Manciple's Tale joined to it. Then, at the end of his
life, when illness or the fear of death, coupled with the
conviction that he should have used his talents for piety
rather than for amusement, suddenly closed down upon
him, he made a definite ending, with the prologue and
tale of the Parson, and the *Retraction*. He had probably
translated the tale earlier, either as a separate work of
devotion or for eventual use in the pilgrimage. There is
no conclusive evidence that he intended the tale of the
Parson (with that of the Manciple) for the return journey. In his desire to make a quick and pious end, he

left various discrepancies unexplained, just as he did between the number of tales promised and those actually written. Such inconsistencies seemed of little importance, however, compared to making his peace with Heaven, and finishing up the whole as best he could. The *Retraction* appears to be his own work, and to reflect deep personal feeling.

It must first of all be emphasized that these problems are all related; that each has to be studied with the others in mind. Many attempts to solve them have failed to take this into account. As we shall see, the *Parson's Prologue,* the *Parson's Tale* and the *Retraction* are closely connected, each with the next, by references and echoes.

The *Manciple's Tale* is usually considered one of the least important in the whole work. It is short, conventional, and in no way especially appropriate to a thieving steward. It has sometimes been thought that it was written early;[1] this conjecture may be true, but of course Chaucer may have done inferior and routine-like writing in his latest years. Possibly he had this story in his desk and utilized it at this point. Had he composed it especially for the Manciple, he would probably have made it suggest more clearly the marked characteristics of that worthy. But whatever is lacking in the tale itself is more than compensated for in its prologue. This is one of the most delightful of all the interludes—rol-

[1] "The Manciple's Tale is proved by its literary technique to have been written long before the period of the Canterbury Tales, probably as a sort of rhetorical exercise" (Manly, *Studies in Philology* XXVIII [1931], 616). "Proved" is strong. However, it makes no difference for the present argument whether the tale is early or late.

licking, dramatic, and vivid. The Cook is drunk. There is no love lost between him and the Host, as the prologue to the earlier *Cook's Tale* shows,[2] and here is Harry Bailly's chance to put him in a tight place by demanding another story, with the heavy penalty of paying all the roadside expenses if he refuses. At this point the Manciple interposes, saying that with the Host's permission he will excuse the Cook from his story. So he is allowed to take the place of the Cook. He has doubtless already had his troubles with the knights of the skewer in his capacity as purchaser of provisions, and is now making things worse with his gibes. But the Host reminds him that he had better be cautious if he does not want some of his own shady practices exposed. So he offers the Cook a drink, which nearly finishes that hero, and then proceeds to tell his tale. The whole prologue gives every evidence of having been written gaily and rapidly, and is certainly in Chaucer's best vein. There is no intimation that the journey is drawing to a close, either at Canterbury or London.

But in the *Parson's Prologue,* which should immediately follow the narrative of the Manciple,[3] Chaucer

---

[2] There seems no valid reason to conclude, as some scholars have done, that Chaucer intended to cancel the Cook's story about Perkyn the Reveller (A 4365 ff.). Of course it is unfinished, but so is the *Squire's Tale.* When the Host says "Is that a cook of Londoun?" he surely does not mean that he does not know that the fellow is a cook, but that the rascal is so drunk as to be scarcely recognizable.

[3] This has been questioned, but without sufficient grounds. In one MS (Hengwyrt) the word "maunciple" in the first line of the *Parson's Prologue* is written over an erasure, and in another (Christ

takes the greatest pains to show, not less than four times, that only one more tale is needed to complete the series. The Host says:

> Lordynges everichoon,
> Now lakketh us no tales mo than oon.
> Fulfilled is my sentence and my decree;
> I trowe that we han herd of ech degree;
> Almost fulfild is al myn ordinaunce.

In calling upon the Parson to speak he says:

> . . . every man, save thou, hath toold his tale.
> Unbokele, and shewe us what is in thy male;
> For, trewely, me thynketh by thy chere
> Thou sholdest knytte up wel a greet mateere.

And the Parson replies:

> I wol yow telle a myrie tale in prose
> To knytte up al this feeste, and make an ende.

Church) the word "yeman" is to be found, and the spurious *Yeoman's Tale* precedes. So it has been conjectured that "possibly Chaucer left the space blank, and the Manciple's name was inserted by the scribe or editor who finally combined the fragments" (Robinson, p. 872, reflecting earlier comments). But why should we give credence to a MS which inserted a tale which Chaucer never wrote, and had to make this plausible, or be disturbed by an erasure in another MS, which *does* show the word "maunciple"? (For a full statement of the MS evidence see Manly and Rickert, *Text of the Canterbury Tales,* IV, 361.) Tatlock, after a thorough discussion, decides that "Chaucer's MSS had *manciple* unless some meddler actually changed the word in it, or unless the original was never copied from but once, both suppositions unlikely. The conceivable supposition that Chaucer left a blank has nothing to be said for it" (*"Canterbury Tales* in 1400," p. 138; see also pp. 122 ff.). Manly and Rickert print "maunciple" in their text.

The pilgrims agree to this arrangement:

> Upon this word we han assented soone,
> For, as it seemed, it was for to doone,
> To enden in som vertuous sentence.

So the plan that each pilgrim shall tell four tales is here suddenly abandoned, whereas in the *Manciple's Prologue* the Host had called on the Cook for the second time.[4] I do not see how we can escape the conviction that in the *Parson's Prologue* we have an abrupt and heavily emphasized decision to throw the earlier scheme overboard. Of course due allowance must be made for possible changes which may have been in Chaucer's mind (and with a temperament as mercurial as his one never knows), but it certainly looks as if he were here trying to give the impression of a completeness which did not exist, trusting that the reader or listener, after so long an interval, would forget the number of pilgrims and the four tales to be given to each, as promised in the *General Prologue*.

Moreover, there are notable changes in tone and subject matter. Jesting and badinage are over when the Parson takes the center of the stage, which is, of course, in part due to his serious character. It is also appropriate that he shall give the pilgrims something edifying, especially if they are approaching Canterbury. In response to the Host's request for a story, he replies that St. Paul reproves those who "tellen fables and swich wrecched-nesse," that he will not sow chaff when he can sow wheat, so he will show the company the way to the

---

[4] See note 2, above.

Heavenly Jerusalem—which he does at great length. His contribution is not a story at all, or in the form of a story; there is nothing narrative about it. This is surprising; nowhere else had Chaucer proceeded in such a fashion. Even the *Melibeus,* heavily didactic as it is and slight as is its narrative interest, does have a plot. It begins:

A yong man called Melibeus, myghty and riche, bigat upon his wyf, that called was Prudence, a doghter which that called was Sophie.

Upon a day bifel . . .

Contrast the opening of the "tale" of the Parson.

Jer. 6°. State super vias, et videte, et interrogate de viis antiquis que sit via bona, et ambulate in ea; et inuenietis refrigerium animabus vestris, etc.

Oure sweete Lord God of hevene, that no man wol perisse, but wole that we comen alle to the knoweleche of hym, and to the blisful lif that is perdurable, amonesteth us by the prophete Jeremie, that seith in thys wyse . . .

This leads to a consideration of penitence, the way to Heaven. The difference between the two is striking. How did it happen that Chaucer here abandoned for the first time his plan that each entertainment of the company should take the form of a story?

It has often been conjectured that he did not make the translation which now stands as the *Parson's Tale.* There are in it no original passages. It ultimately depends upon a sermon on penitence and a tract on the Seven Deadly Sins, both of the thirteenth century. Both were popular; it is not known upon what version or versions the translation is based or whether the two were already united or first here combined. Conceivably someone else may have been responsible for the English version. This is, however, contradicted by the fact that it *is* in the Canterbury collection, by echoes in Chaucer's undoubted work, and by many bits of characteristic phraseology.[5] Those who think it unlikely that this sort of thing would have interested Chaucer should reread the *Melibeus,* the authenticity of which is established by the opening lines of the *Monk's Prologue* immediately following. And there may well be a very special reason why this penitential material had a particular appeal for him at the very end of his life.

Granted that he did translate it, did he intend it for the Parson? In one of the most authoritative of recent discussions, this is questioned.[6]

Two things . . . are obvious. One is that we lack any account of the jolly supper promised in the Prologue as the conclusion of the Pilgrimage, and that the CT as we have it ends on a very different tone. One may, therefore, be allowed to doubt whether Chaucer himself was responsible for the choice of the two prose treatises which are put together to form PsT and for the melancholy Retraction which, instead of the promised celebration at the Tabard, closes the collection of tales. [A conjecture follows as to the way in which the two treatises were joined.] It therefore seems possible that the person—probably a priest—who composed the Retrac-

---

[5] "Present opinion is decidedly in favor of the authenticity of the whole work." Robinson, p. 873.

[6] Manly and Rickert, *Text of the Canterbury Tales,* IV, 527. Quoted by permission of the Chicago University Press.

tion found the two prose treatises among Chaucer's papers
and consolidated them for the purpose of supplying the missing prose tale promised by the Parson.

I think that this view is wrong. Against it is the fact
that the tale told by the Parson fits his promises in his
prologue remarkably well, even to similarities of language. He says that its purpose is

> To shewe yow the wey, in this viage,
> Of thilke parfit glorious pilgrymage
> That highte Jerusalem celestial.

The opening passage of the tale lays stress on the way
that a Christian should follow. "Of whiche *weyes,* there
is a ful noble *wey* and a ful convenable, which may nat
fayle to man ne to womman that thurgh synne hath
misgoon fro the righte *wey* of *Jerusalem celestial.*" [7] It
looks, then, as if Chaucer in writing the *Parson's Prologue* had very much in mind the opening of the discourse to follow. The assumption, adopted without question in the passage just quoted, that the person who
composed the *Retraction* was not Chaucer, is not held,
as we shall see in a moment, by the best authorities.[8]
A further objection to Chaucer's assignment of the present tale to the Parson has been that that worthy priest
speaks of it as "myrie" (l. 46), which would be "com-
ical." [9] But this neglects the fact that "merry" in the
fourteenth century and, indeed, long after often meant,
not "jolly," but "pleasant," "satisfying." The yard where

[7] Italics, of course, mine.

[8] Earlier Manly himself was less sure; see his edition of the *Tales,*
1928, p. 657.   [9] *Ibid.,* p. 656.

Chanticleer strutted was "mery" (B² 4156); Arcite looks on the "myrie day" (A 1499). "Merry England" was a pleasant land, not one where people were always laughing. The word was often used of religious emotion. Thus, the King James Version renders James, V, 13 "Is any among you afflicted? Let him pray. Is any merry? [Vulgate *aequo animo*] Let him sing psalms." The "pleasant" effect produced by moral instruction upon men of Chaucer's day must never be forgotten.[10]

Why do we "lack any account of the jolly supper promised in the Prologue"? Why is it that a gloomy and devotional mood prevails? The reason seems to be, as I have already suggested, that at this time Chaucer had experienced a religious crisis, so that he not only had no heart for amusement, but was even willing to abandon completely the pleasant earthly joys of the pilgrimage, and wind it up abruptly. Illness or fear of imminent death, with the medieval fires of hell glowing luridly in the distance, may well have driven him to make his peace with Heaven, to disavow past literary "sins," and to make such amends as were possible.

It may, perhaps, be replied that the Parson is, after all, only speaking in character when he preaches a sermon and urges penitence, and that this would be particularly appropriate if the pilgrims were just approaching the shrine of St. Thomas. It may be further urged that since

[10] For further illustrations see the *New English Dictionary*, sub *merry*, A 1–2. The *Melibeus* is called "murye" (B² 964), but here, as in the phrase "a litel thyng in prose," Chaucer the pilgrim was apparently saying to the Host "Well, if you don't like my little joke about Sir Thopas, here is something long and edifying enough for you!"

Chaucer appears to have skipped about in the filling in of the drama and in writing stories for the journey, he may have arranged the prologue and tale of the Parson for the end of one stage, intending to complete the rest in his usual fashion later. Again, the translation of penitential material certainly did not necessarily imply a change of heart; such material was highly esteemed for its own sake and need not be given a personal application. With these points in mind, some of us may be inclined to doubt that the pious ending of the *Tales* was due to Chaucer's own contrition.

Before reaching a decision, the *Retraction* ought to be considered with special care. If we believe that Chaucer wrote it, and meant what he wrote in all sincerity—which I believe to be the case—I do not see how we can escape the conclusion that he was also, in the prologue and tale of the Parson, so closely connected with the *Retraction,* trying to make amends for those worldly portions of the earlier narrative, as well as for other works to which a strict churchman might very well take exception.

The available evidence seems strongly in favor of the authenticity of the *Retraction.*[11] It does not look like a piece tagged on by an outsider; it is closely connected in thought, by the three well-recognized stages through which the medieval sinner passed on the path of amendment, with the Parson's long discourse. The final prayer

[11] See Robinson, p. 880, for references. His conviction is that "on the whole there is no sufficient reason for rejecting the *Retractation.*"

that the poet may be granted "grace of verray penitence,
confessioun and satisfaccioun" echoes "Now shaltow
understande what is bihovely and necessarie to verray
perfit Penitence. And this stant on three thynges: Con-
tricioun of herte, Confessioun of Mouth, and Satisfaccioun." [12] When we read the opening of the *Retraction,*
"Now preye I to hem alle that herkne this litel tretys or
rede," we are, I believe, listening to the voice of Chaucer
himself. The textual evidence supports this: the *Retraction* is to be found as a conclusion to the *Parson's Tale*
"in all MSS. thus far described which have the immediately preceding part of the *Parson's Tale* unmuti-
lated." [13] It has been maintained that it contains "inac-
curacies" which point to possible composition "by some
pious friend—perhaps a monk of Westminster—upon
suggestions furnished by [Chaucer]." [14] This conjecture
(which was later accepted almost as fact) [15] is not well
founded. The reasons why this is so have already been
set forth in Chapter III. According to the narrowly
pietistic view of the *Retraction,* a writer should devote
the talents which God has given him to works of moral-
ity and devotion, and particularly avoid those celebrating sexual love. This was a theological commonplace
in the Middle Ages; it explains why apparently innocent poems are disavowed in the *Retraction.* The tales
that "sownen into synne" appear, then, to include those

[12] Group I, 106 ff.; Robinson, p. 274, col. 1.
[13] Robinson, p. 1015.
[14] Manly, *Canterbury Tales* (1928), p. 658.
[15] See above, p. 152.

dealing with sex not only in its coarser aspects, but in its romantic aspects as well.[16]

But apologizing was a literary habit in the medieval period, and we have seen that there is good reason to believe that Chaucer's excuses for his less edifying stories are not to be taken at their face value. Why, then, may not the *Retraction,* even if genuine, be a mere literary device, a convention, not expressing real contrition or a sincere desire to disavow work displeasing to the Church? Did Chaucer, like Prince Hal, carefully arrange a later repentance, and cheerfully go on sinning?[17]

I do not know of any way of proving that this was not the case. No one can tell what was passing through Chaucer's mind and heart. But the burden of proof lies with those who think the *Retraction* insincere or conventional. Dr. Thomas Gascoigne, the learned chancellor of the University of Oxford, in his *Dictionarium theologicum* (1434–1457) wrote: "Thus Chaucer before his death frequently cried out 'Woe to me, woe to me, because I can neither recall nor destroy those things which I sinfully wrote concerning the base and sinful love of men for women, and which now will be con-

---

[16] See above, pp. 83 ff. The reference to the *Legend of Good Women* as "the book of the xxv ladies," which does not square with the facts, "might be due to various causes, and is surely not reason enough for rejecting Chaucer's authorship of the *Retractation*" (Robinson, p. 881). Most MSS have xxv; Robinson reads xix in his text, as did Skeat (*nynetene*).

[17] As, for example, was suggested by Miss Hammond, MLN, XLVIII (1933), 515.

tinually circulated among men.'"[18] Kittredge advised those "who have found incredible the story of Chaucer's death-bed repentance told by Dr. Thomas Gascoigne" to read the will of Sir Lewis Clifford.[19] Many instances of strong religious repentance accompanied by disavowal of literary work have been collected. Contrition hit men hard in times when eternal punishment was believed the sequel to earthly sins. The experience of Boccaccio is noteworthy. When he was nearly fifty years old, he became morbidly penitent, and indeed there was much in his past life to repent. The story of the visit of the Carthusian monk, who warned him that he had not long to live and that he ought to give up poetry, is too well known to need repetition. Fortunately Petrarch gave his terrified friend wise counsel and comfort. In the remaining years of his life Boccaccio produced much secular work in Latin, which strict churchmen might regard with an indulgence impossible to extend to his earlier amatory poems and prose work in the vernacular. This repentance contrasts strikingly with his apologies at the end of the *Decameron,* which, as we have seen, were almost openly mere lip-service to convention.[20]

[18] Spurgeon, *Chaucer Criticism and Allusion,* I, 43; Manly, *Canterbury Tales* (1928), p. 657.

[19] MP, I (1903), 13. The passage from the will is conveniently accessible in Manly, *loc. cit.* In all probability, Chaucer's word "retracciouns," and perhaps the writing of his formal expression of penitence, go back ultimately to the *Retractiones* of St. Augustine. On this general subject see the article by Tatlock, "Chaucer's *Retractions,*" PMLA, XXVIII (1913), 521–529.

[20] Compare Edward Hutton, *Giovanni Boccaccio,* London, 1910, pp. 198 ff., and above, p. 77.

There is an unusually close parallel, which I do not think has been noted, in the life of La Fontaine. Like Chaucer, he was a fashionable and celebrated poet at a court steeped in convention. At the age of seventy-one he was seized by a severe illness. His confessor, before giving him absolution and the last sacrament, required him to disavow his licentious *contes,* and prevailed upon him to burn an unfinished comedy. The *contes* in question were somewhat similar in character to the medieval fabliaux. As a further evidence of contrition, La Fontaine set himself to translating the Penitential Psalms. In similar fashion Chaucer, in the *Retraction,* expressed repentance for having devoted himself to secular writing, but gave thanks for his rendering of the *Consolation of Philosophy* of Boethius and for "legendes of seintes, and omelies, and moralitee, and devocioun," and finally wound up his great collection of stories with translated penitential material. A man of his highly emotional and imaginative temperament might well have gone to lengths of disavowal of earlier work which we find hard, in days of a more liberal theology, to understand. The Church was always pleased by open acts of contrition, and would have welcomed such a document as the *Retraction* all the more because of its uncompromising tone. The Middle Ages seldom did things by halves; the extreme was to be expected.[21]

[21] Odd resemblances, of course accidental, may be observed between the *Canterbury Tales* and the very interesting *Metamorphoses* of Lucius Apuleius (second century A.D.). The incidental stories in the *Golden Ass*—to use the more familiar title—are narrated by different persons, male and female, in the course of the travels and adven-

If we do take the view that we have here a true reflection of Chaucer's state of mind, various difficulties which have puzzled scholars disappear immediately. In the *Manciple's Prologue* it is morning ("by the morwe" H 16), but after the very short tale which follows, and the Parson is called upon to speak, it is late afternoon.

> By that the Maunciple hadde his tale al ended,
> The sonne fro the south lyne was descended
> So lowe that he nas nat, to my sighte,
> Degreës nyne and twenty as in highte.
> Foure of the clokke it was tho, as I gesse,
> For ellevene foot, or litel moore or lesse,
> My shadwe was at thilke tyme, as there,
> Of swiche feet as my lengthe parted were
> In sixe feet equal of proporcioun.
> Therewith the moones exaltacioun,
> I meene Libra, alwey gan ascende,
> As we were entryng at a thropes ende;
> For which oure Hoost, as he was wont to gye,
> As in this caas, oure joly compaignye,
> Seyde in this wise: "Lordynges everichoon,
> Now lakketh us no tales mo than oon."

---

tures of the Ass; they vary in length from a short episode to the long and elaborate tale of Cupid and Psyche. Most of them belong in the category of Milesian Tales, the fabliaux of antiquity, and some passages are certainly offensive to modern ideas of decorum. The whole closes with the conversion of the hero, who is in some degree identifiable with the author, to the cult of Isis, through whose intervention he has regained human shape. "The account of the religious experience is no fiction, but a glimpse into the genuine and the deepest experience of a human soul." A. B. Hawes, *Citizens of Long Ago,* New York, 1934, p. 89.

And again the Host says "But hasteth yow, the sonne wole adoun." It seems clear that Chaucer is emphasizing the point that there is time for only one more tale on that day, and reinforcing the point by astronomical detail, although this does not square with what stands in the *Manciple's Prologue*.[22] It is just what might be expected in an effort to put an abrupt end to the collection. Furthermore, the much disputed question as to whether he wrote the tales of the Manciple and the Parson for the journey to Canterbury or for the return is seen to be no question at all. If, as I believe, he did neither, but was intent on finishing things up, his insistence at the very beginning of the *Parson's Prologue* that it was late afternoon, with little time left on that day, fits in very neatly with his repeated assertion that every pilgrim had told his tale.

It has been thought that indications of place favor

[22] There is no doubt that "foure of the clokke" is the right reading. The astronomical description of the low height of the sun puts ten o'clock quite out of the question. Chaucer was not always careful to have his time scheme free from inconsistencies, but his astronomy in any given passage does work out correctly. Probably some scribe or scribes felt that the frequently found emendation (for such it appears to be) to ten o'clock would remove the inconsistency between the two prologues, or, as has been plausibly suggested, "in the ancestral MS the time was written with an arabic numeral 4, but the fifteenth-century form of 4 is easily mistaken for the roman numeral x; and this mistake occurred here. The same error occurred elsewhere in these MSS, e.g., in F 386 the correct reading is also 'foure'; MSS Ch, Hg, and Py have arabic 4, twelve MSS have roman x, and twenty-seven spell out 'ten'; the others, including El and Gg, spell out 'foure'." Quoted from the prospectus of the Manly and Rickert edition; cf. also IV, 528.

the conclusion that Chaucer intended the tales of the Manciple and the Parson for the return journey. The scene of the *Manciple's Prologue* is "a litel toun which that ycleped is Bobbe-up-and-doun, under the Blee, in Caunterbury weye," almost certainly to be identified with Harbledown, by the forest of Blean near Canterbury. When the Parson is summoned to speak, the pilgrims are just "entryng at a thropes ende." But there is no village between Harbledown and Canterbury, though there may, perhaps, have once been a little hamlet there, no longer existing.

If pilgrims bound for Canterbury have reached "Bobbe-up-and-doun" . . . they are all but at the end of their way. A quarter of an hour of easy riding will bring them to their journey's end. From the top of Harbledown hill they would see spread before them the goal of their pilgrimage. It seems most unlikely that Chaucer, with his keen sense of actuality and his certain familiarity with the road that leads through Canterbury to Dover, should have thought of his pilgrim company as beginning a new tale with the destination already in sight. It is quite inconceivable that he should have thought that between "Bobbe-up-and-doun" and Canterbury there was time both for the Manciple's Tale and the long discourse of the Parson.[23]

I do not think that this difficulty need be taken too seriously. We have earlier seen that it is impossible to fit the tales by length into any rational time scheme. In any

[23] R. K. Root, "The Manciple's Prologue," MLN, XLIV (1929), 494. Root concludes that "the Manciple's Tale was intended for the beginning, and the Parson's for the conclusion of the homeward journey."

case, how could this be done in the present instance? The Host urges the Parson to be "fructuous, and that in litel space," and asks him to hurry, as the sun "wol adoun" —and then the man of God tells by far the longest of all the tales! It seems possible, indeed, that the line "As we were entryng at a thropes ende" was put in for the sake of a rhyme to the technical term "ascende" which closes the astronomical explanation. A necessary and unusual word demanded a rhyme to fit.

It will now be clear why Chaucer wrote a longish prologue for the Parson. We might think that if he was anxious to finish up abruptly, with a tale exhorting penitence, and with a personal recantation, he would have introduced the Parson briefly, and proceeded straightway to what he had on his mind. But there were other things to be considered. It is generally agreed that certain portions of the *Tales* were in circulation while he was still alive. He must have known that there would be eagerness after his death to assemble these and to add others not already given out. Many of the stories point moral lessons—those of Man of Law, Second Nun, Pardoner, Monk, Prioress, Clerk, Manciple, and Nun's Priest. Why should these be sacrificed? They do not "sounen into synne," no matter what we think the phrase means. There was no reason why a work which had occupied the poet's chief literary energies for more than ten years should be sacrificed utterly. Was it not better, since an end must be made, to give this plausibility and dignity? Most of all it was necessary to emphasize three things: that there was time for only one more story; that everyone but the Parson had told his tale; and that moral teaching might now be expected.

So the gay and buoyant poet of the *General Prologue* has become the frightened penitent of the *Retraction,* ready to forswear both the lusty humor of the tavern and the decorative romance of the castle hall. It is hard to realize this, but I think that we must. Repentance apparently came very late, probably in the last year of Chaucer's life, but not "on his death-bed," as is often conjectured. The *Parson's Prologue* does not sound like a death-bed production. There is some evidence that he was employing romantic conventions up to about a year before he died. The *Compleynt to his Purs,* with "its humorous adaptation of the language of a lover's appeal to his mistress," does not look like the work of a man who had renounced love poetry. Its Envoy "can be very precisely dated. It must have been written between September 30, 1399, when Henry was received as king by the parliament, and October 3, when Chaucer received the royal grant of an additional stipend of forty marks." [24] He died, according to our best knowledge, on October 25, 1400.

Chaucer's general attitude toward religion, prior to the change which we may infer at the end of his life, may be gathered with reasonable accuracy from his writings and from what we know of his career. He must have been a good regular churchman, otherwise he could hardly have maintained his position at court and in governmental affairs. To antagonize the ruling powers

[24] Quotations from Robinson, pp. 980–981.

would have been the end of his appointments. There was plenty of heresy in England, sometimes mixed up with politics, but to meddle with it was risky business. No man of Chaucer's wide experience and clear vision could have been blind to the scandals in the church at the time when the *Canterbury Tales* were written—the Great Schism (1378 on), the corruption of the minor clergy and of ecclesiastical parasites, the indecent scramble in higher places for money, preferment, and power. The effect of all this upon the English people had been marked and bitter. But it would be a great mistake to think of Chaucer as a Wicklifite or a Lollard, or as anticipating the ideas of the Reformation. In the *Tales* he strikes at the corruption of typical individuals, never at doctrines. Nothing in his ironical portraits suggests the moral indignation of Langland. Castigation of obvious abuses was a very different matter from questioning, as Wiclif did, the fundamentals of dogma. The Host's disrespectful words to the Parson, "O Jankin, be ye there? I smelle a Loller in the wynd" (B 1172-3) do not suggest sympathy with that sect. The Lollards disapproved of pilgrimages.[25]

In one respect, however, Chaucer's attitude, until the very end, does point forward to the new age just beginning, with its conviction that man is a being of worth and ability in his own right and able to some extent to

[25] G. M. Trevelyan, *England in the Age of Wycliffe,* New York, 1899, p. 131. On Chaucer's religion see the able article by E. P. Kuhl, "Chaucer and the Church," MLN, XL (1925), 321-338. There is also a good discussion by Tatlock, "Chaucer and Wyclif," MP, XIV (1916), 257-268.

mold his own destiny. Human existence, as the Pilgrimage reveals it, is no gloomy interlude between the cradle and the grave for men irrevocably doomed except through special grace. The spirit of the *Tales* often seems close to that of Rabelais, not because of occasional indecorum, but because of the conviction that life is good and joyous. The reason why there is so little reflection of the problems and distresses of the day is, I believe, that these were deliberately avoided. There is no suggestion of acute national anxiety and depression;[26] the sun is always shining on the road to Canterbury. There are, indeed, moments of seriousness and expressions of bitterness (which must not be taken as Chaucer's own feelings) from some of the pilgrims, for no picture of life would otherwise be complete, but the prevailing mood is that of a holiday, of a company bent on forgetting the sorrows and vexations of everyday existence.

This is what makes the closing in of the shadows in the *Retraction* so striking. The *Tales* end in a huddled and inconsistent fashion, with a frightened disavowal of pleasure, of genial storytelling, of the delights of love and romance, and with a final cry of penitence and remorse. The grim rather than the comforting aspect of

[26] "The Londoners, timid as hares and nervous as mice, sought conflicting counsel on all sides, peered into dark places, and began to mistrust their own strength, and despair of resistance as though the city were on the point of being taken. . . . Not one Frenchman had yet set foot on a ship, no enemy had put to sea, yet the Londoners were as fearful as though all the surrounding country had been conquered, and they saw the enemy before their gates." Thomas of Walsingham, *Historia Anglicana,* quoted by D. Hughes, *Illustrations of Chaucer's England,* London, 1918, p. 142.

medieval religion was at this time uppermost in the consciousness of the poet; it chilled his brave spirit and broke his courage. Like any poor sinner, he could only cry *mea culpa!* and do what he could to reconcile himself to its stern dictates. Let us hope that it brought him peace of mind at the end, but let us rejoice that it came no sooner!

❧ BIBLIOGRAPHY

This brief selection from the many commentaries on ·Chaucer and his times has been made with particular reference to the subject matter and purposes of this book. Various other important studies dealing with special topics are suggested in the footnotes above.

EDITIONS OF THE CANTERBURY TALES

W. W. Skeat, Vol. IV in The Complete Works of Geoffrey Chaucer, 6 vols., with supplementary volume containing Chaucerian and Other Pieces, Oxford, 1894–1897. Usually known as the Oxford Chaucer. Text, with brief introduction, appendix, and glossary, reprinted in one volume, Oxford, 1895, etc.; called The Student's Chaucer.

A. W. Pollard, Chaucer's Canterbury Tales, 2 vols., London and New York, 1894. A very pleasant edition to read; brief notes at the foot of the page; now (1949) out of print and in need of modification in the light of recent research.

A. W. Pollard, in The Works of Geoffrey Chaucer, Globe edition, London, 1898, etc.

J. M. Manly, Canterbury Tales by Geoffrey Chaucer, New York, 1928. Not a complete text; expurgated, and much omitted. Valuable material in the Introduction and Notes, but in need of modification and revision. Text in the Ellesmere sequence.

F. N. Robinson, Complete Works of Geoffrey Chaucer, Boston, etc., 1933. Excellent text and full critical apparatus. Of special use to the advanced student. Text in the Ellesmere sequence.

J. M. Manly and E. Rickert, The Text of the Canterbury Tales, 8 vols., Chicago, 1940. Of great value to the specialist, but not adapted to the general reader.

To the question often asked, which edition of the *Tales* is best suited to reading for literary enjoyment, a satisfactory answer is hard to give. In Chapter I above the importance of having a complete text, even though only certain portions are read, is explained and emphasized. The volume in the *Oxford Chaucer* has clear type and broad margins, but is expensive, bulky and not easy to obtain. The section in the *Student's Chaucer* suffers from the necessary compression of the complete works into one volume. The same is true of the *Globe Chaucer* and of Robinson's excellent edition. Skeat's complete text of the *Tales* is reprinted in the "Modern Library," New York, 1929, with glossary, but without line numbering or section divisions. The Introduction is not recommended. Of the many editions of selections, that by Manly (1928) is, perhaps, the most complete, but the sequence of tales adopted in this, as in Robinson's text, is of questionable desirability for the general reader.

BIBLIOGRAPHIES AND CONCORDANCE

E. P. Hammond, Chaucer; a Bibliographical Manual, New York, 1908.

D. D. Griffith, A Bibliography of Chaucer 1908–1924, Seattle, Wash., 1926.

J. E. Wells, A Manual of the Writings in Middle English, 1050–1400, New Haven, Conn., 1916 (and later supplements).

J. S. P. Tatlock and A. G. Kennedy, A Concordance to the Complete Works of Geoffrey Chaucer, Washington, D.C., 1927.

W. E. Martin, Jr., A Chaucer Bibliography, 1925–1933, Durham, N.C., 1935.

LITERARY CRITICISM

R. K. Root, The Poetry of Chaucer, Boston, etc., revised edition, 1922.

É. Legouis, Geoffroy Chaucer, Paris, 1910. English translation, London, 1913.

G. L. Kittredge, Chaucer and His Poetry, Cambridge, Mass., 1915.

R. D. French, A Chaucer Handbook, New York, 1929, 1946.

J. L. Lowes, Geoffrey Chaucer and the Development of His Genius, Boston and New York, 1934.

H. R. Patch, On Rereading Chaucer, Cambridge, Mass., 1939.

SPECIAL SUBJECTS

J. Bédier, Les Fabliaux, 4th edition, Paris, 1925.

J. S. P. Tatlock, The Development and Chronology of Chaucer's Works, Chaucer Society, Second Series, No. 37, London, 1907. Still indispensable, but should in some cases be supplemented by later research. See especially the same author's "The Canterbury Tales in 1400," PMLA, L (1935), 100–139.

G. M. Trevelyan, England in the Age of Wyckliffe, 4th edition, London, 1909.

É. Mâle, Religious Art in France: XIII Century, translated from the third French edition (revised and enlarged), London and New York, 1913.

F. Watt, Canterbury Pilgrims and Their Ways, London, 1917.

G. G. Coulton, Chaucer and His England, 3d edition, London, 1921.

J. J. Jusserand, English Wayfaring Life in the Middle Ages, revised edition, London, 1925.

C. F. E. Spurgeon, Five Hundred Years of Chaucer Criticism and Allusion, 3 vols., Cambridge, Eng., 1925. A wealth of quotation and comment, with full bibliographical information.

W. C. Curry, Chaucer and the Mediaeval Sciences, New York, 1926.

G. R. Owst, Literature and Pulpit in Medieval England, Cambridge, Eng., 1933.

J. M. Manly, Some New Light on Chaucer, New York, 1926. Useful as a commentary; its conclusions should be taken with reserve.

G. G. Coulton, Medieval Panorama, New York and Cambridge, Eng., 1938.

W. F. Bryan and G. Dempster (editors), Sources and Analogues of Chaucer's Canterbury Tales, Chicago, 1941. Detailed essays by various writers; very important.

M. Bowden, A Commentary on the General Prologue to the Canterbury Tales, New York, 1948.

E. Rickert and others, Chaucer's World, New York, 1948.

TRANSLATIONS

Those who use this book will wish to draw their conclusions from the original text. In general, translations do not seem as necessary or desirable as is often maintained. Very little preparation is needed to read Chaucer with fair comprehension. Though much will be missed, it seems better to miss it from his own words than to miss his own flavor from a dilution. For those who desire a translation, however, the following may be recommended. There is a good deal to be said for those in verse. Chaucer's characteristic grace and music are likely to vanish in being reduced to prose. In lyrical passages, such as the prologues of the Prioress and Second Nun, this is particularly unfortunate; in *Sir Thopas* much of the point of the satire of the degenerate verse-romances is lost; the grave melody of pathetic passages, as the Ugolino of Pisa episode in the *Monk's Tale,* fades away. However, the choice between verse and prose is a matter of opinion. Anything that aids in understanding Chaucer should be welcomed.

Those who prefer verse will find the following satisfactory. In each of them the text is complete and unexpurgated, and in the *Oxford Chaucer* sequence.

J. U. Nicholson, Geoffrey Chaucer; Canterbury Tales, with illustrations by Rockwell Kent and an Introduction by Gordon Hall Gerould, New York, 1934.

F. E. Hill, The Canterbury Tales, London and New York, 1935.

For prose renderings the reader may turn to the following.

The second follows the sequence of the *Oxford Chaucer;* it is expurgated, and much is omitted, but a great deal of Chaucer's other work is included in the volume. There are charming illustrations in color by Warwick Goble. Lumiansky's rendering, which follows the Ellesmere sequence, is complete for the tales included, but those of the Monk (except the *Ugolino of Pisa*), Prioress, Parson, and Chaucer in the *Melibeus* are omitted. Of the colored illustrations impressions may vary. The simplicity of Chaucer's style is well preserved, and a useful feature of the book for those unacquainted with Middle English is the inclusion of the *General Prologue* and *Nun's Priest's Tale* in the original.

R. M. Lumiansky, The Canterbury Tales of Geoffrey Chaucer, New York, 1948.

J. S. P. Tatlock and P. MacKaye, The Modern Reader's Chaucer; the Complete Poetical Works, New York, 1912.

✒ INDEX